felicia lidia radu
beatrice abala

team handball
101

techniques, tactics and drills

BLOOMSBURY

LONDON · NEW DELHI · NEW YORK · SYDNEY

Bloomsbury Sport
An imprint of Bloomsbury Publishing Plc

50 Bedford Square
London
WC1B 3DP
UK

1385 Broadway
New York
NY 10018
USA

www.bloomsbury.com

BLOOMSBURY and the Diana logo are trademarks of Bloomsbury Publishing Plc

First published 2015

British Library Cataloguing-in-Publication Data
A catalogue record for this book is available from the British Library.

ISBN: Print: 978-1-4729-0180-4
ePDF: 978-1-4729-0182-8
ePub: 978-1-4792-0181-1

2 4 6 8 10 9 7 5 3 1

Typeset in DIN by Saxon Graphics Ltd, Derby
Printed and bound in Great Britain by CPI Group (UK) Ltd, Croydon CR0 4YY

To find out more about our authors and books visit www.bloomsbury.com. Here you will find extracts, author interviews, details of forthcoming events and the option to sign up for our newsletters.

CONTENTS

FOREWORD

The main aim of *101 Team Handball: Techniques, tactics and drills* is to provide a useful tool for coaching, teaching (or self learning) a game which is in the Summer Olympic Games programme and which is quickly increasing in popularity. The fact that all players can score goals (including the goalkeeper) makes the game highly appealing to all ages.

The book covers the fundamental skills that every player needs to master in order to play handball successfully. The 101 drills focus on all these skills and present helpful coaching points to avoid common mistakes.

The major theme of the book is the technical and tactical aspects of the game for both defence and attack. A chapter is dedicated to the goalkeeper and their training and you will also find a general overview of the game in terms of history, rules to play the game and the referee's signals.

This book came about from our experience at various levels of the game – we played in the same team at professional level in the 1st National League in Romania – and from coaching the game at junior and senior level. Our intention is to share some of our knowledge and to further contribute to the development of this beautiful sport. We hope this book will give you a few useful ideas that can easily be applied in practice.

Enjoy playing handball!

KEY TO DRILLS

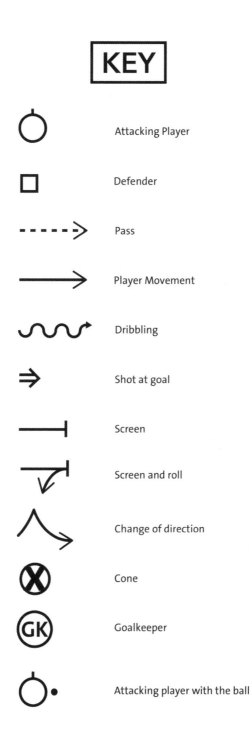

KEY

⭕	Attacking Player
⬜	Defender
- - - ▷	Pass
⟶	Player Movement
〰⟶	Dribbling
⇒	Shot at goal
⊤	Screen
⊤↓	Screen and roll
⋀↘	Change of direction
Ⓧ	Cone
ⒼⓀ	Goalkeeper
⭕•	Attacking player with the ball

KEY TERMS

4-metre line the mark on the court within each 6-metre semicircle which shows how far away from the goal the goalkeeper is allowed to move when defending a 7-metre throw (penalty throw).

6-metre line the semicircle area in front of each goal that indicates the goalkeeper's restricted zone. This is an area where the field players are not allowed. Also called 6-metre goal area.

7-metre line the line drawn on court seven metres in front of each goal, which indicates the spot where the penalty throws are taken.

9-metre line an interrupted line drawn 3 metres outside the 6-metre semicircle in front of each goal; also called 9-metre semicircle.

Back (right back and left back) situated in the right and left back areas of the team offence around the 9-metre semicircle. Ideally each team will have a right-handed player in the left back position and a left-handed player in the right back position.

Centre back this is the player who usually plays in the middle of the offence and who creates and dictates the play in both offence and defence. Also called playmaker.

Goalkeeper the player who is defending the goal. They are the only player allowed inside the 6-metre semicircle in front of each goal. The goalkeeper is also allowed to touch the ball with any part of their body when they are inside the 6-metre area.

Crossover a tactical move in offence performed by two or more attackers who switch places to confuse a defender. Also, a term given to the individual tactical action performed while dribbling the ball – the attacker changes the direction of the dribble by moving the ball in front of his body from one side to the other.

Fast break a fast attack that creates an easy scoring opportunity before the defence can get organised. Also called counter-attack.

Extended fast break the continuation of a fast break. After the fast break is launched, the defence sometimes has time to stop an initial shot attempt and slow down the offence; this is when the attackers try to use the momentum in their favour by using 2–3 quick and sharp passes to surprise the defenders.

Fake a feint performed with the aim of deceiving an opponent into making a wrong move. The most common fakes are: pass fake, shot fake, change of direction fake.

Feints see **fake**.

Free throw a throw that is awarded against a team whose player commits a foul or a rule violation. It is taken from the place where the foul or the violation was committed.

Line player see **pivot**.

Pivots the player who plays on the 6-metre semicircle when their own team is in offence and tries to create spaces for his teammates to score easily. Also called line player or circle runner.

Rebounding the ball the individual tactical action performed by both attackers and defenders with the aim of recovering a ball that is bouncing back onto the playing area after a shot has been taken (bouncing off the defenders or off the post).

Screen tactical combination in offence performed by two attackers. One of them will set a screen for the other by placing his body in the path of a defender with the aim of stopping them from guarding his direct opponent.

Time-out a 1-minute break during the game requested by a team's coach by placing a green card on the table in front of the timekeeper. A time-out can also be requested by the referee, following a 2-minute suspension, a disqualification or an exclusion.

Wall a collective tactical action performed by 2 or more attackers that aims to facilitate a jump throw to goal from a distance over the defenders.

Wing the player who is situated on the wing, close to the corner of the court. He can throw the ball from a much narrower angle than the backs. Each team has a right wing and a left wing – they are the players that run the most during the game.

Zone defence a defensive playing system in which the defending players cover areas of the court rather than marking individual players, as is the case in man-to-man defence situations.

Ximena Cedeno of Ecuador in action during a match between Venezuela and Ecuador in Women's handball as part of the XVII Bolivarian Games Trujillo 2013 in Chiclayo, Peru : (photo by Mathhias Kern/Bongarts/Getty Images)

OVERVIEW OF RULES

Handball is a popular, dynamic and exciting game. Over 15 million people practise this sport worldwide; in Europe it is the most popular sport after football. In general terms, the game is a combination of football, basketball and polo. Here is a quick overview of the most important aspects of the game.

Playing court

The playing court (see Figure 1) is rectangular, measuring 40 metres long and 20 metres wide; it is made of two goal areas and the playing area. The longer boundary lines are called side lines and the shorter ones are called goal lines (between the two vertical posts of the goal) or outer goal lines (on either side of the goal). With the exception of the goal lines, which are 8 centimetres wide, all other lines are 5 centimetres wide.

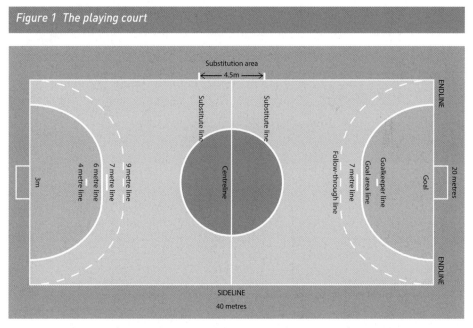

Figure 1 The playing court

The goals are 2 metres high and 3 metres wide (see Figure 2). Each goal must have a net.

Figure 2 The goal

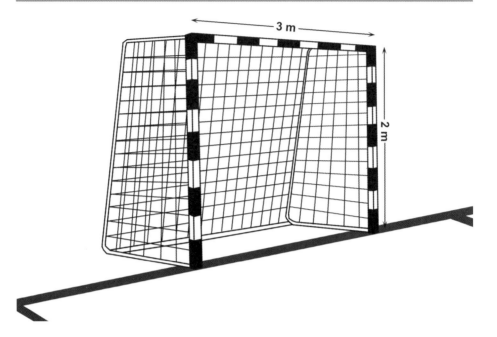

The field lines form part of the spaces they mark out.

The 6-metre goal-area line indicates the goalkeeper's restricted zone; field players are not allowed in this area (with the clear intention of scoring, if the players are attacking, or with the intention of creating an advantage in defence, if the team is in defence).

The 9-metre line (or free throw line) is an interrupted line, drawn 3 metres outside the goal-area line (3 metres away from the 6 metres line).

The 7-metre line (penalty line) is a 1 metre long line, directly in front of the goal. It is parallel to the goal line and 7 metres from the goal line.

The goalkeeper's restraining line (the 4-metre line) is 15 centimetres long, directly in front of the goal; it indicates the point up to which the goalkeeper is allowed out of the goal line when defending 7-metre throws (penalty throws).

The centreline (halfway line) divides the court into two equal parts, each court belonging to a team (at the end of the first half, the two teams change courts).

The substitution line (a segment of the side line) for each team extends from the centreline to a point situated at a distance of 4.5 metres from it. This point of the substitution line is marked by a line which is parallel to the centreline and which extends 15 cm inside the side line and 15 cm outside the side line (inside and outside the court).

A goal is scored when the entire circumference of the ball has passed over the entire width of the goal line (if the thrower, a teammate or a team official did not commit any violation of the rules before or during the throw) – see Figure 3. The goal line referee will confirm a scored goal with two short whistle blasts.

Figure 3 Scoring a goal

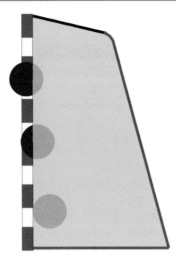

NO GOAL

NO GOAL

GOAL

Positions on court

Goalkeeper (GK) – this player's main task is to defend the goal; they are the only player allowed to touch the ball with any part of their body and the only player allowed in the semicircle area.

Right wing (RW), left wing (LW) – these players throw the ball from a much narrower angle than the backs and take part in the build-up of their team's attack. The two wings move around the court most during the match; they need to be first in attack after the opposite team lose the ball. Ideally, your team would have a right-handed player playing on the left wing and a left-handed player playing on the right wing.

Right back (RB), left back (LB) – typically the team's shooters who play in the two areas around the 9–metres semicircle. It is ideal to have a right-handed player playing on the left side and a left-handed player playing on the right side.

Centre back (CB) – the player who dictates play in both defence and attack; they should create numerous opportunities that lead their team to score goals. The centre back is sometimes called the playmaker.

Line player (LP) (or pivot; also called circle runner) – this player runs on the semicircle trying to create spaces for his teammates so they can score easily. This player also tries to create blocks (to set screens) for his teammates, usually for the main scorers of the team.

Substitutes – a substitution is allowed at any moment, without limit and time stoppage. There are seven substitutes in each handball team, but they cannot enter the court and play until the player who is being substituted is off the court.

To see the positions for each player see Figure 4.

Figure 4 Position of players on court

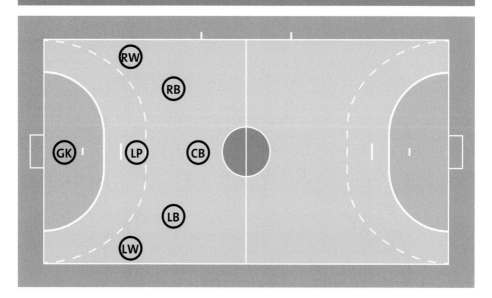

Playing time

The playing time for teams of players aged 16 and above is two halves of 30 minutes, with a half-time break of 10 minutes.

The playing time for youth teams is two halves of 25 minutes for the 12–16 age group and 2 halves of 20 minutes for the 8–12 age group. If a game is tied at the end of normal playing time, extra time is played, following a 5-minute break. The extra time comprises two halves of 5 minutes, with a 1-minute half-time break.

If there is still a tie after this first period, a second period of extra time is played following a 5-minute break. This is also 2 halves of 5 minutes, with a 1-minute half-time break.

If the game is still tied, 7-metre throws will be used as a tiebreaker (similar to a penalty shoot-out in football). Five players from each team will make a throw each, alternating with players from the other team.

Final signal

Play starts with the referee's whistle and the ball must be passed (the player with the ball is not allowed to dribble or to execute other actions, but he must pass the ball to another player).

Play ends with the automatic final signal from the public clock, or from the timekeeper. The timekeeper monitors the playing time according to the regulations of the competition.

If no such signal comes, the referee whistles to indicate that play is over. If there is no public clock with an automatic final signal, the timekeeper will use a table clock or a stopwatch and he will end the game with a final signal.

Unsportsmanlike behaviour that takes place before or simultaneously with the final signal (for half-time or for the end of the game, or during extra time) will be penalised, including if the resulting free-throw or 7-metre-throw cannot be executed until after the whistle.

Similarly, the throw must be retaken if the final signal (for half-time, or for the end of the game or extra time) is heard precisely when a free-throw or a 7-metre-throw is being taken or when the ball is already in the air.

Time-out

Each team benefits from one 1-minute time-out in each half of the regular playing time. A time-out is requested by the coach by placing a green card on the table in front of the timekeeper. When the time-out is over, the game is resumed when the referee blows his whistle.

The referees can also request a time-out following a 2 minutes' suspension, a disqualification or an exclusion.

The ball

The handball is usually made of leather or a synthetic material. It must be spherical and the surface should not be slippery or shiny.

The ball size (circumference and weight) differs according to the category of teams as set out by the International Handball Federation (IHF) regulations:

58–60 cm and 425–475 g (IHF size 3) for male and male youth teams (over age 16);

54–56 cm and 325–375 g (IHF size 2) for women, female youth (over age 14) and male youth teams (age 12–16);

50–52 cm and 290–330 g (IHF size 1) for female youth (age 8–14) and male youth teams (8–12).

Basic rules

There are seven players in each team: six court players and a goalkeeper. The aim of the game is to score as many goals as possible in the goal of the opposite team. Each goal scored is awarded one point.

Touching the ball with the foot or the leg below the knee is sanctioned – referred to as 'foot'. The goalkeeper is the only player allowed to touch the ball with the feet when defending the goal (see also Rules Relevant to Goalkeeper, page 9).

Any player is allowed to make three steps with the ball in hand; more than that is an infraction known as 'too many steps', or sometimes 'travel'.

On receiving the ball, any player may hold the ball for three seconds, otherwise he will be penalised for 'too many steps'.

The court players are not allowed in the goal area, the semicircle area in front of each goal. The majority of the action of play in handball is played between these two semicircles on the handball court.

If the ball goes off the court, completely crossing the side line, or crossing the outer goal line, the situation is called 'out' (out of bounds). A throw-in is awarded and the ball is thrown back into play from the side line by the team that did not hold possession of it, or by the team whose player did not touch the ball on its exit from the playing space. The throw-in is taken from where the ball crossed the side line and the player taking the throw must stand with one foot on the side line.

An 'offensive foul' occurs when an attacking player hits a defender using their shoulder or chest.

The player who executes a multiple dribble and catches the ball several times between dribbles commits the rule violation known as 'double dribble'.

The 7-metre throw

A 7-metre throw is awarded when:

- the defence commits a foul against their opponents to prevent a clear chance of scoring, or
- an offensive player is about to score and a defensive player holds the attacker's arm(s) or commits a foul to stop the goal.

The 7-metre throw must be taken as a shot-on-goal. The player taking the throw should have both feet behind the 7-metre line. The player should not cross or touch the line until the ball has left their hand.

Match officials/referees

There are four handball officials: a scorekeeper, a timekeeper and two referees. Both referees have equal authority: one of the referees monitors the activity of the players in the goal area while the other identifies the violations committed in the field, between the two 9-metre semicircles (free throw) area. The referees are responsible for how the game unfolds and make sure that the rules are followed.

Player substitutions

A court player can be substituted by a teammate from the side line – this change must take place over their own team's substitution line.

A faulty substitution will be penalised with a 2-minute suspension for the guilty player. If more than one player from the same team is proven guilty of faulty substitution in the same situation, only the first player that committed an infraction will be penalised. The game is restarted with a free throw for the other team. If an additional player enters the court without a substitution, or if a player illegally interferes with the game from the substitution area, there will be a 2-minute suspension for the player, thereby reducing their team's players on court for 2 minutes.

If a player enters the court while serving a 2-minute suspension, he will be given an additional 2-minute suspension. This suspension will begin immediately, so the team will be further reduced on the court during the overlap between the first and the second suspension.

In both cases, the game is restarted with a free throw for the opponents.

The equipment

Every court player in a team must wear identical kit. The combinations of colours and the design for the two teams must be clearly different from one another. The goalkeeper must wear a colour that distinguishes them from the court players of both teams, and from the goalkeeper of the opposing team.

The players must wear numbers that are at least 20 cm high on the back of the shirt and at least 10 cm high on the front. The numbers used should be from 1 to 99. A player who switches between the positions of court player and goalkeeper must wear the same number in both positions. The colour of the numbers must contrast with the colours and design of the shirt.

The players must wear sports shoes. Players are not allowed to wear objects that could be dangerous to other players; this includes face masks, bracelets, watches, rings, visible piercing, necklaces or chains, earrings, glasses without restraining bends or with solid frames, or any other objects that could be dangerous. Players who do not meet these requirements will not be allowed to take part until they have corrected the problem.

Passive play

Players are not allowed to keep the ball in a team's possession without making any obvious attempt to attack or to shoot at the goal. Similarly, it is not permitted to repeatedly delay the execution of a throw-off (the throw that starts the game from the centre of the court at the beginning of the match, or that re-starts the game after a goal is scored), free throw, throw-in, or goalkeeper's throw for his own team. This is considered passive play and will be penalised with a free throw against the team in possession of the ball, unless the passive tendency stops. The free throw is executed from the spot where the ball was when play was interrupted.

Fouls

The following actions are permitted during play:

- using an open hand to play the ball away from the opponent;
- using bent arms to make (and maintain) body contact with an opponent in order to monitor and follow the opponent;
- using the body to obstruct an opponent, even if the opponent is not in possession of the ball.

For fouls or infractions committed by the defenders between the free-throw line (9-metre semicircle) and the goal area (6-metre semicircle), the offensive players put the ball back into play from the free-throw area from the spot where the infraction was committed. Infractions occurring between the free-throw areas of the two court halves will be penalised and the ball is put back into play by the team who won the ball possession, from the spot where the infraction was committed (similar to a football free kick).

The following actions are not permitted during the play:

- pulling or hitting the ball out of the hands of an opponent;
- blocking or forcing away an opponent using arms, hands or legs or using any part of one's body to move the opponent or to push him; this includes the dangerous use of elbows, both standing and in movement;
- holding the body or uniform of an opponent, even if the opponent is free to continue playing;
- running or jumping into an opponent.

Warnings

A warning can be given for:

- a foul or infraction against an opponent which is not under the handball regulation;
- fouls which are to be punished progressively;
- unsportsmanlike conduct by a player or team official: physical and verbal expressions that are incompatible with the spirit of good sportsmanship.

An individual player should not be given more than one warning and a team should not be given more than three warnings; thereafter, the punishment should be at least a 2-minute suspension. A player who has already had a 2-minute suspension should not subsequently be given a warning. No more than one warning in total should be given to the officials of a team. The referee shall give a yellow card to the player who is found to commit a further foul, or to the team official, by holding the yellow card up.

Suspension

A suspension (2 minutes) shall be given:

- for a faulty substitution: when an additional player enters the court the wrong way or enters the court before the other teammate is off the court;
- for repeated fouls that are punished progressively;
- for repeated unsportsmanlike conduct on the court or outside the court;
- as a consequence of disqualification (if a player or a team official has been disqualified, immediately another player is suspended for a period of 2 minutes).

Disqualification

A disqualification shall be given:

- for fouls which endanger the opponent's health;
- for a third suspension given to the same player;

- for unsportsmanlike conduct by any of the officials of the team, after they have previously received both a warning and a 2-minute suspension.

A disqualification of a player or a team official is always for the entire remainder of the playing time. After calling a time-out, the referees should clearly indicate the disqualification to the guilty player or official, and to the timekeeper/scorekeeper by holding up a red card.

Rules related to goalkeeper play

The goalkeeper is allowed to:

- touch the ball with any part of his body in defence inside the goal area;
- move with the ball in his hands inside the goal area;
- leave the goal area without the ball, but while outside his area he becomes subject to rules that apply to the field players;
- score from his area (from goal to goal).

The goalkeeper is not allowed to:

- endanger the opponent while in act of defence;
- leave the goal area with the ball in his hands, as this leads to a penalty shot for the opposing team;
- try to get the ball that is stationary or rolling outside of the goal area, while he is inside the goal area;
- take the ball into the goal area when he is already outside the goal area.

Handball is fast, dynamic and easy to learn because the movements are natural and encountered in daily life: walking, running, jumping, throwing and variations of these movements.

Poland's Karol Bielecki (l) attempts a shot on goal during the 24th Men's Handball World Championships 3rd place match between Spain and Poland at the Lusail Multipurpose Hall in Doha, 2015 (photo by MARWAN NAAMANI/AFP/Getty Images)

BRIEF HISTORY OF HANDBALL

Handball around the world

The game of handball is a fast and physically demanding team sport in which natural moves and basic skills such as running, jumping and throwing are combined with speed, power, coordination and endurance. All major joints of the body (ankles, knees, elbows and wrists) are constantly used to successfully execute a wide range of individual and team actions that are performed with various levels of effort (maximal effort, sub-maximal, medium alternated with very short break moments).

Handball is a relatively new sport. Some believe that the game had its origins in Germany, but other countries also had games which were very similar to handball. In modern times, countries such as Denmark, Germany and Sweden are considered the handball pioneers. These countries are the foremost handball nations, alongside Russia, France, Norway, Hungary, Romania, Spain and Korea.

Handball has also developed in Africa as one of the most popular sports alongside football. Egypt, Tunisia, Algeria, Angola and Congo, to name just a few, are countries where great success has been achieved at African and international level.

Handball has been an Olympic event for men since the 1972 Munich games and for women since the 1976 Montreal games. Other developments in the sport include the creation in 1991 of the European Handball Federation (EHF) in Berlin. Today its headquarters are in Vienna, Austria.

Additionally, the World Championships took place every four years until 1990, but a 2-year cycle was introduced in 1995. In 2002, the first European Beach Handball Championship was played in Cadiz, Spain. According to the International Handball Federation (IHF), which was founded in 1946, handball is currently played in 199 countries and the number of teams worldwide amount to approximately 800,000.

Handball in the UK

At world level, handball is controlled and managed by the International Handball Federation (IHF), which is the world governing body. At European level, the EHF governs the game, while at national level all handball activities are run by a National Federation (NF) or a National Governing Body (NGB) – in England's case this is England Handball (EH). Some of the main activities for which England Handball is responsible include: organising the national league and various age group competitions; players' and clubs' affiliation; coaches, referees and match officials' development; and volunteer recruitment.

Figure 5 Governing bodies of Handball

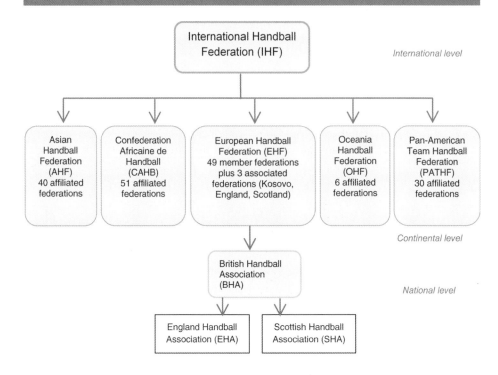

Figure 5 Governing bodies of Handball

HANDBALL TECHNIQUES AND SKILLS

The techniques in a game of handball comprise a variety of specific motor actions necessary to accomplish attacking and defensive tasks. Technique is closely connected to tactical advantage while physical qualities underpin the technical elements. All these components of training depend on each other; however, the technique is the main factor of the game.

Drills used to teach the game need to appeal to the players to inspire a love of handball. During practice, the aim is to replicate real game situations as far as possible to achieve a rhythm of execution, so that applying these skills in the actual game is done efficiently.

The learning process is gradual with general objectives established for each training level/stage. The complexity of the drills used in the technical training of children and beginners should increase gradually until they eventually replicate the complexity of a game. An important characteristic of children's drill training is acquiring and improving these fundamental skills.

In modern handball, when assessing a player's technical execution, the coach must observe the following:

- the position of the player's body before and during the movement;
- the trajectory and range of movements;
- the whole movement tempo and the execution speed of the technical procedure.

Handball game techniques can be acquired following certain steps:

- Learn the technique in easier conditions, usually without any opposition. The first phase of teaching a particular technique involves analysing it. For example, to practise catching the ball with two hands, two players are placed face-to-face and pass the ball to each other, catching with two hands. If errors occur, the coach can explain and demonstrate the correct execution, focusing on repeating the procedure until any errors are eliminated.
- Practise using alternatives to replace the opponent (e.g. dribble between cones with changes in direction, jump throw after taking off from the bench, dive shot and landing on a mat, etc.).
- Practise with a passive opponent (attacker or defender). The purpose is to practise the technique correctly, but also to take into account the presence of the opponent. The coach can change the tasks continuously (e.g. players switch from attacker to defender, and vice versa), in order to maintain the interest and efficiency of the lesson.
- Practise with a semi-active or active opponent. The main aim is to ensure technique is executed with continuity, coordination and consistency.

Gradually conditions similar to the game will be introduced into practice – i.e. the player practises the technique against an active opponent who plays within the rules in order to stimulate the player to react similarly to a game-related situation.

- The improvement and consolidation of the technical elements by learning complex drills replicating game situations. For example, the left wing runs towards the goal, receives the ball from the goalkeeper, executes a dribble, feints the opponent and throws to goal. This can also be practised with an active defender trying to stop the attacker.

Techniques/skills for defence

The aim of practising defensive techniques is to improve a player's ability to protect the goal, skills that will ultimately help determine the final score of the game. When playing in defence, all players adopt a basic position which can be high (see Figure 6), medium (see Figure 7) or low (as in Figure 8).

Figure 6 Defenders adopting a high fundamental position

Figure 7 Defenders (in white) adopting a medium fundamental position

Figure 8 Defender (number 26) adopting a low fundamental position

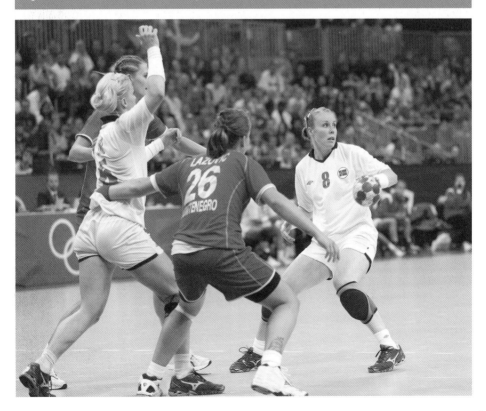

For a defender to develop an effective game, they should know all the technical skills needed and have good physical training so they can adapt and use these skills against their opponents. Running; standing and moving forward; stopping; change of rhythm and direction while running; falling back; sudden turning; lateral movement; arm motion independent from leg motion; torso movements in bending and turning around; jumps – these are all general skills that every defender should possess and apply in game situations.

Specific skills needed by the defender

- Getting the ball from the opponent who is dribbling through a front, side and behind the back move.
- Getting a ball that is being held in a player's hand.
- Getting the ball by intercepting it.
- Blocking throws to goal.
- Blocking the ball using the foot.
- Defending against an opponent by using the chest.

Getting the ball from the opponent using a move from the front
The attacker's action of penetrating towards the goal – if the attacker is dribbling, the defender can steal the ball by intercepting mid-bounce using one or both hands.

Getting the ball using a move from the side
Closely marking the opponent is an action specific to the defender, in order to respond to the rapid attacking penetration move. To steal the ball from the opponent through a dribble, the defender places their hand under the opponent's dribbling hand. In this way, the defender will be the first to touch the ball or prevent the opponent from catching the ball.

Getting the ball using a behind-the-back move
The defender gets the ball when the attacker turns his back to the defender or when his positioning on court favours this action. When the ball is bounced, the defender places their hand in the trajectory of the ball, rebounding the ball towards them or a teammate.

Getting the ball that is being held in a player's palm
Hitting over the ball, snatching it or committing any violent act in order to get the ball from the opponent is penalised by the referee with a free throw. However, the defender still has an option to steal the ball balanced by the attacker in their palm – the defender is allowed to use his open palm to take the ball.

Intercepting the ball
The defender follows the trajectory and the passing direction of the ball and anticipates the action of the receiving attacker they are defending. The player intercepts the ball mid-trajectory by moving rapidly toward the opponent and catching the ball before it gets to the attacker. The ball interception does not

involve the knowledge of any special skills, apart from anticipating the actions of the attacker; this skill comes with experience in matches.

Blocking throws to goal

Defenders block throws by the backs or by the centre back from the free-throw area. The defender puts his arms together and jumps with the shooter, thus blocking the trajectory of the ball toward the goal. This technique can be executed individually in a one-on-one situation (see Figure 9) but also simultaneously by 2 or 3 defenders trying to stop a shot (see Figure 10).

Figure 9 Defender trying to block the shot in a one-on-one situation

Figure 10 *Several defenders blocking a shot*

Blocking shots thrown from 9 metres over the defenders

Defenders of the goal stand with legs slightly flexed, arms stretched up and close together, ready to block a throw. The defenders use their arms to block the trajectory of the ball. If the shooter jumps in the air to throw the ball, the defender should jump with their arms extended.

Blocking the ball using the foot

Balls that bounce off the floor at knee height or below cannot always be blocked using the arms. The defender can prevent a goal by interposing his foot – or even a hand – to block the ball. Despite this option being available to defenders, they must remember that balls blocked with the foot will lead to a penalty (9 metres throw) being awarded to the opposition if the ball was touched with the leg below the knee, or to a suspension if the foot was lifted off the floor.

Defending an opponent by using the chest (tackling the opponent)

This technique is allowed in the rules, but only if performed properly. To tackle an opponent the defender approaches and, without committing a foul, slightly pushes them using their chest to prevent them from controlling the ball, and then throwing the ball towards the goal (see Figure 11).

Figure 11 Player using her chest to defend against an attacker

Drills and exercises for defenders

The techniques a defender needs to acquire include the ability to move easily, and to react rapidly to their opponent's moves.

getting the ball using a move from the front

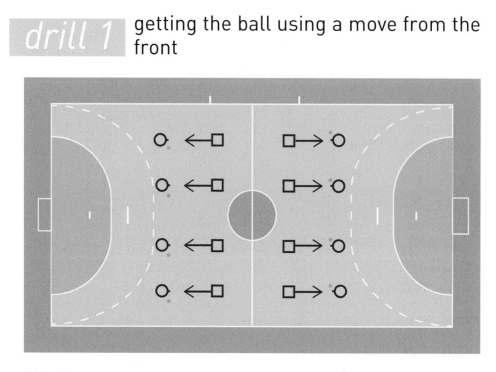

Objective: To practise winning the ball facing the attacker.

Description: The players work in pairs, facing each other at 2–3 metres away. One player dribbles the ball on the spot while the other uses their palm to intervene in the trajectory of the ball, taking the ball away from the player dribbling it. Change roles after 4–5 goes (or after a couple of minutes).

Coaching points:
- use an open palm to steal the ball;
- do not bump into the attacking player;
- try to keep the ball alive by continuing to dribble it once the ball has been stolen.

Common errors:
- the player attempting to steal the ball collides with the attacker, committing a foul;
- the player trying to steal the ball holds the ball in his palm rather than dribbling it.

getting the ball using a move from the side

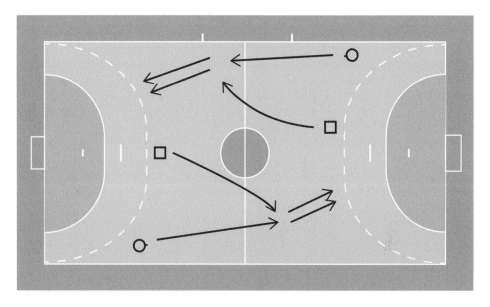

Objective: To practise winning the ball approaching from the side.

Description: This drill is executed without the ball in order to practise synchronising runs with the opponent. The attacker runs towards the goal while the defender, who starts 6–8 metres away, turns, catches up with the attacker, then runs closely alongside.

Coaching points:
- advise the defender to get back into the defensive position, so that he is slightly ahead of the attacker or runs side by side;
- once close to the attacker, the defender should maintain some distance so as not to collide with them.

Common errors:
- the defender does not get back into defence quickly enough;
- the defender runs straight into the attacker, committing a foul.

Progression: Perform the drill with the ball; the attacker dribbles the ball and the defender comes from the side to steal the ball.

pig in the middle

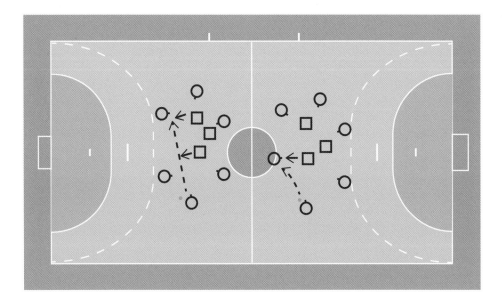

Objective: To learn how to intercept the ball in a team situation.

Description: 6–8 players form a circle with 2–3 defenders inside. The players around the circle (attackers) pass the ball amongst themselves, while those in the centre move in order to intercept the ball. Any player within the circle who catches or touches the ball is replaced with the player who just passed it.

Coaching points:
- try to anticipate the direction of the pass and who is it aimed at;
- sprint towards the ball during its flight and use one or both hands to intercept it, trying to get control of it.

Common errors:
- players do not correctly anticipate the trajectory of the ball when they want to intercept it;
- players react to passing fakes and commit themselves too early, moving out of their position and allowing attackers an easy pass.

Progression: Perform the drill again, but this time the player with the ball is not allowed to pass to the teammate who is immediately next to him on either side of the circle.

drill 4 blocking the balls on goal

Objective: To prevent the ball from reaching the goal.

Description: The defender stands on the 6-metre line and the attacker starts with the ball on the 9-metre line. The attacker's task is to throw the ball to the goal line. The defender must use his arms to block the ball from reaching the goal.

Coaching points:
- extend arms upwards above the head to create a tall wall in front of the goal;
- keep arms fairly close together;
- try to anticipate the direction of the shot and use the hands to stop the ball.

Common errors:
- defender turns their back to the attacker at the moment of the shot;
- arms are not fully extended upwards;
- arms are not close together.

Progression: Two attackers are placed on the 9-metre line, 2 metres apart. The defender is on the 6-metre line and moves from one attacker to the other, depending on the ball movement between them. After 3–4 passes, the attackers must make a throw on goal which the defender has to block.

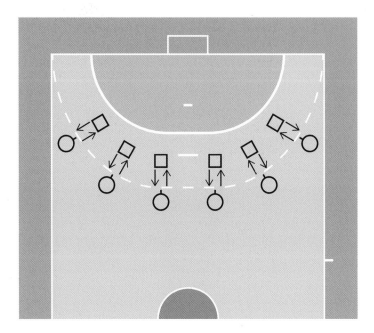

Objective: To develop quick reactions to an attacker with the ball.

Description: The defenders are placed on the 6-metre line, while the same number of attackers are in the free throw area. The attackers pass the ball between themselves and the defenders come out one by one and attack the ball. After the ball is passed from the opposite attacker, the defender withdraws to their original position at the 6-metre line.

Coaching points:
- react quickly and move out from the 6-metre line as soon as the attacker in front of you has received the ball;
- get back on the 6-metre line immediately, as soon as the attacker has passed the ball.

Common errors:
- defenders hesitate to move towards the attacker with the ball, or make only one step instead of moving convincingly towards the attacker;
- defenders get back on the 6-metre line and touch this line, which is not allowed.

Progression: The speed of the pass will increase so that the defenders have to move quicker towards the attacker.

Other defending-specific practices:

- running backwards in the direction of motion when the attackers lose possession of the ball and return to their own half of court (i.e. getting back in defence)
- running backwards (facing the direction of the run), eyes to the ball;
- sideways motion, specific to the defence, executed on the 6-metre line or on the 9-metre line, depending on the defensive system adopted – active movement of feet and of arms above the head;
- exiting/getting to the ball and getting back on defence;
- change of direction.

Techniques/skills for attackers

As with defence, there are specific technical elements that every player should be aware of when playing in attack. One of the most important elements is the basic 'ready' position – this is specific to the players holding the ball or to those preparing to receive it. The player who receives the ball has their upper body (shoulders and head) turned towards where the ball is coming from, with arms stretched to receive the ball, while their knees are slightly flexed. The attacker holding the ball and who is ready to pass will have his ball-holding hand behind him so that he gets more power into the pass. The leg opposite to the throwing hand will be placed in front, facing the direction of the throw. Usually, the most commonly seen positions are:

The basic position specific to the pivot.

Offensive play occurs when, while playing in defence, the team gains possession of the ball and then moves from their half into their opponents' half – i.e. the defenders become the attackers. This whole process involves movements with and without the ball. All attackers should be able to perform basic movements on court such as running, change of direction, lateral moves, penetration, turning around, stopping, jumping – all performed without the ball in order to get open to receive the ball. They also need to be able to execute specific actions with the ball: dribbling, passing and catching, use of fakes, throwing towards goal.

drill 6 catching the ball

Objective: To practise catching the ball correctly and efficiently.

Description: It is strongly recommended to always catch the ball with two hands irrespective of the height of the pass or the direction the ball comes from. However, sometimes players catch the ball using one hand only.

Coaching points:
- the player who is catching the ball with two hands will have his arms out, palms facing the ball. By touching the ball with both hands simultaneously, he will flex his elbows backwards and inwards, in order to absorb the force of the ball's transmission;
- fingers are spread out and slightly flexed but not excessively tensed.

Common errors:
- incorrect position of the upper limbs when catching the ball, arms are not ready, tensed hands, fingers not spread out;
- lack of attention – receiving player is not looking at the teammate who is passing the ball;
- fear of a ball that is being passed too powerfully.

drill 7 holding the ball

Objective: To hold the ball securely.

Description: While in offence, the ball can be held either with one hand or with two hands. The first situation is used just before a player throws a one-handed pass, while the second is recommended especially when receiving the ball.

Coaching points:
- have your palms wide open with fingers spread out;
- bring the ball close to your chest in order to protect it.

Common errors:
- players do not hold the ball properly, and so drop it;
- players do not use both hands to safely catch the ball.

Handling the ball
After catching the ball, the attacker can handle the ball with various actions until the moment he passes it, dribbles it or throws it. For example, he could take the ball from overhead to hip level for a special pass, and he could do this by rotating his arm forwards, backwards or sideways. These movements will be executed within the limit of the rules, by respecting the three steps rule, or the three seconds rule for example.

drill 8 dribbling the ball

Attacking player who commits the rules violation called 'leading'

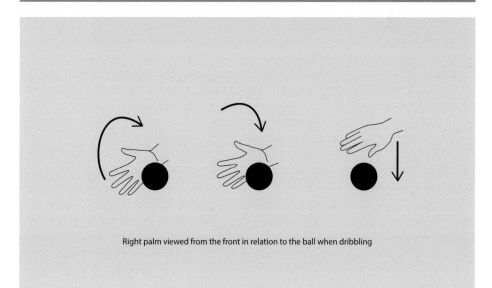

Right palm viewed from the front in relation to the ball when dribbling

Objective: Dribbling the ball is the technical element specific to the attack, through which a player moves with the purpose of entering into the opponents' space, without being afraid of making too many steps.

Description: The number of times the ball hits the floor will determine the type of dribble: a single dribble is when the attacker bounces the ball once only and after catching it performs another technical element such as a pass to a teammate or a throw to the goal; a multiple dribble occurs when the attacker will continuously dribble the ball while advancing on the court or in a stationary position. The dribbling action can also be classified by the height of the dribble – high, medium or low – and the direction of movement, e.g. dribble while changing direction in order to avoid opponents by changing and alternating the dribbling hand.

Coaching points:
- players should not commit the rules violation 'leading' (when the player dribbling the ball places the hand under the ball and by rotating the wrist brings the hand to the top of the ball);
- during the multiple dribble, the ball is sent forwards onto the floor and slightly to the side diagonally;
- the line starting from the palm must be perpendicular to the floor, with the ball on this imaginary line, and the hand always on top of the ball;
- running is coordinated with the execution of the dribble.

Common errors:
- the player dribbles in front of his legs instead of diagonally;
- the ball is bounced with a significant force, rebounding above the waist or even above the shoulder – this is when the player loses control of the ball;
- while bouncing the ball with the palm perpendicular to it, the pushing force is not sufficient enough to make the ball bounce off the floor at a reasonable height (waist height is usually recommended). This will therefore force the player to commit 'leading', e.g. he will have to place his palm under the ball to lift it up so that he can dribble again;
- lack of coordination between the leg action and that of the hand that bounces the ball.

multiple dribble

Objective: To develop dribbling skills.

Description: In groups of 4–5 players a multiple dribble is executed in a straight line. Player 1 in each group is dribbling towards the opposite queue, then passes the ball to the first player in that queue and joins the back of that queue.

Coaching points:
- keep your head up while dribbling;
- dribble the ball to the side, and not in front of your legs.

Progression:
- increase the distance between the queues;
- change speed and rhythm when dribbling.

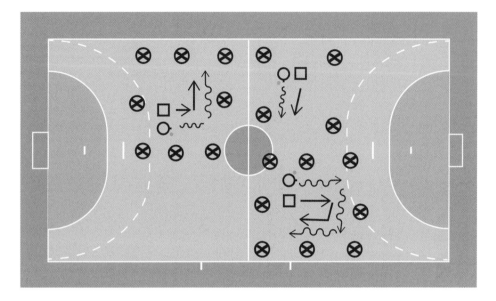

Objective: To develop dribbling skills under pressure.

Description: In pairs, dribble while fighting off the opponent – the defender attempts to take the ball out of the dribble executed by the attacker. Each pair has a limited space marked by cones where they perform the drill. The attacker tries to dribble the ball for 30 seconds (or 1 minute, etc.) and they change roles afterwards.

Coaching points:
- do not dribble the ball too far away from your body;
- to protect the ball, dribble it with the hand furthest from the defender.

Progression: The drill can be played as a 2 v 2 game in the same limited space, or increase the space.

drill 11 dribble between the cones

Objective: To develop accuracy in dribbling technique.

Description: A multiple dribble is performed while passing in and out of the cones – the attacker needs to switch the dribbling hand in front of each cone. The drill can be performed at walking speed initially. Then the speed can be increased – dribble while jogging.

Coaching points:
- make sure you alternate the dribbling hand each time you pass a cone;
- keep your head up while dribbling.

Progression: Defenders can be used in place of cones; they can initially be passive, or semi-active and just pretend they want to steal the ball when the attacker is passing.

drill 12 dribble relays

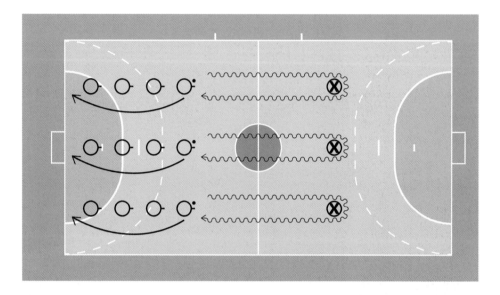

Objective: To practise passing while dribbling.

Description: In teams, Player 1 dribbles towards a cone, round it without stopping the dribbling action and quickly dribbles the ball back before passing to Player 2.

Coaching points:
- players must catch the ball with both hands when dribbling round the cone;
- passes must be accurate – at chest level, powerful, with a flat trajectory.

The chest pass

Objective: Passing is the technical skill that allows the players to move the ball between them while attacking the opposite goal.

Description: Passes can be classified as basic passes or special passes. The chest pass, the bounce pass and the jump pass are considered as being fundamental to the game of handball. The special passes include: pronation pass; supination pass; pushed pass; deviated or touched pass; two hands pass (rarely used in the modern game); lob pass; lob pass over the 6-metre semicircle; behind the back pass; over the shoulder pass. All of them can be performed while having one or both feet on the floor, but also during a jump in the air.

Coaching points:
- the ball should be passed at chest height – the safe area for catching the ball is between the chest and the top of the head;
- the shoulder opposite to the throwing arm must be facing towards the goal or towards the direction of pass in order to protect the ball and to inject more power into the pass – see below;
- the arm holding the ball should remain extended after the pass and the shoulders should be on the same line;
- when a player passes to a moving teammate, the ball should be thrown slightly ahead of the player;
- passes on the move are accompanied by normal running or sometimes by sidestepping.

One hand pass (shoulder pass)

Common errors:

- the player passes the ball below the knee level – this makes catching the ball very difficult;
- low-speed passes, too soft or too strong passes, and passes far from the safety space, i.e. chest and shoulders;
- there is no follow through after the pass and there is no step forward into the pass;
- the player passes with the elbow very close to the body, touching the side of the body;
- the player passes with two hands – although this is not a major mistake, this type of pass is very rarely used;
- passing behind a player who is running forward.

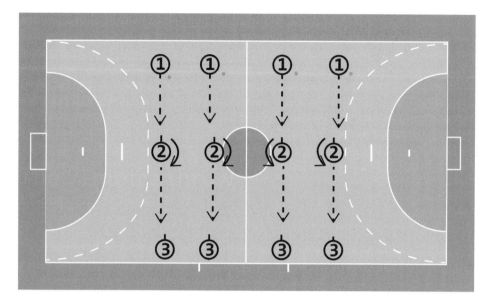

Objective: To practise passing quickly in a line.

Description: Players are positioned in groups of 3. Player 1 has the ball and passes the ball to Player 2 who, as soon as they receive the ball, turns around so that they face Player 3 and pass to them. Player 3 then passes the ball back to Player 2 who pivots again to face Player 1. This can be repeated a number of times before players rotate positions.

Coaching points:
- execute a full 180 degrees pivoting move when you receive the ball so that you face the player you are passing to;
- accuracy of passing – flat pass, powerful enough to reach the destination at above shoulders level.

Progression:
- change the type of pass, such as a bounce pass;
- increase the distance;
- introduce a defender.

drill 15 — passing around the 9-metre semicircle

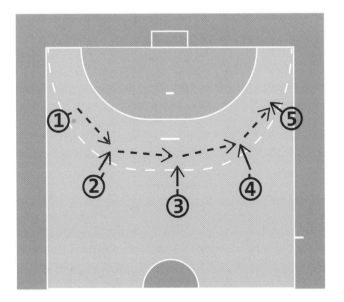

Objective: To practise accurate passing at speed.

Description: Attacking players are grouped in 5s around the semicircle. Player 1 passes the ball to Player 2, who passes it to Player 3 and so on until the ball gets to Player 5 who reverses the direction of the ball.

Coaching points:
- advise players to step towards the ball when the pass is directed to them;
- flat, sharp passes are needed – do not pass the ball too low (at feet level) or too high (above head height).

Common errors:
- players remain still when they receive the ball;
- players do not catch the ball properly and the passing action slows down.

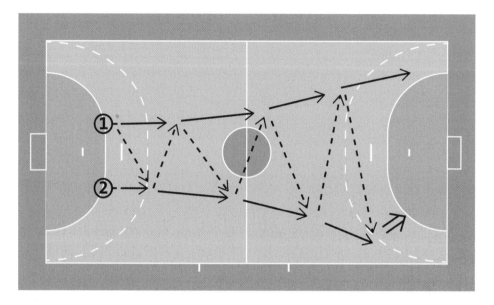

Objective: To develop accurate passing at varying distances.

Description: Work in pairs, with one ball between two. Player 1 passes the ball to Player 2 who returns the pass to Player 1 and so on. After each pass, the player starts running forward but then goes wide, increasing the distance between them.

Coaching points:
- do not stay close to each other – increase the distance between the players after each pass (go forward and wide);
- accuracy of passes is vital as the distance increases.

Common errors:
- players stay too close to each other;
- passes are not accurate.

Feints and changes of direction

Feints and changes of direction are deceiving moves used by the attacking player to get open or to get past the defender, with or without the ball. The pass feint, goal throw feint and jump feint are the most common types. The pass feint is followed by an attacking action: a pass, dribble, moving feint or by a throw. The goal throw feint can be followed by an actual throw at goal, a pass or a dribble.

drill 17 simple and complex feints

Attacker fakes a change of direction towards the right and then starts to move to the left

Attacker beats the defender and throws to goal

Attacker prepares the shot after beating the defender, and finalises the action with a jump shot to goal

Objective: To practise sequences of direction changes and feints to fool the opponent.

Description: Changes of direction and movement feints can be performed with or without the ball and can be simple or multiple fakes. When performed with the ball, the attacker changes direction and moves the ball over the defender (while rotating the arm that is holding the ball), then a quick dribble is followed by catching and throwing to goal.

Coaching points:
- the right leg is facing forwards and slightly to the side for right-handed players (the left-handed will do the opposite);
- the attacker begins the feint by lifting the arm with the ball;
- the ball is then moved over the defender, before a dribble or a goal throw is executed after getting past the opponent;
- the attacker protects the ball from the opponent by using the body.

Progression: Another way of getting past the opponent is performing a fake pass, quick change of direction followed by a jumping step and finish by throwing the ball.

drill 18 feints in threes

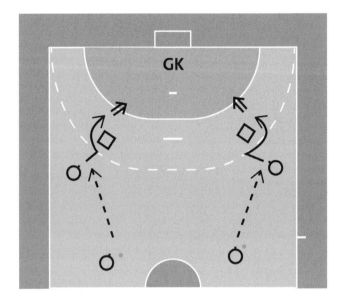

Objective: To practise the change of direction before a shot at goal.

Description: Players work in groups of three – one is the attacker with the ball, one is a defender and is situated on the 9-metre semicircle, and the third player is another attacker. The player with the ball passes it to his teammate who performs a change of direction and passes the defender on the outside moving towards the side line/baseline. The action finishes with a shot at goal. After a few minutes, the players change roles so that everyone gets to practise the feint and change of direction before throwing to goal.

Coaching points:
- the ball should be caught at chest height while changing direction;
- the torso will be slightly tilted in the direction of motion;
- between the second and third step, the athlete must decide what to do next;
- the fake move has to be convincing in order to beat the defender;
- stay strong with the ball while you perform the move.

Progression: the defender, initially passive, becomes active.

change of direction and passing feint

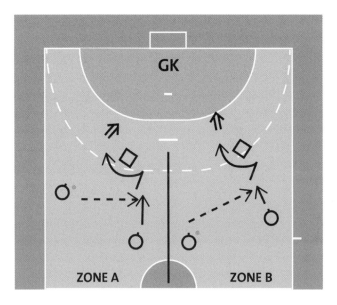

Objective: To develop a convincing passing feint following a change of direction.

Description: Players practise on both sides of the court so that they perform a final move towards the outside/zone A and also towards the inside/zone B. In turns, attackers with the ball will perform a change of direction and will then combine this with a passing fake. Initially defenders can be passive, and then semi-active and active..

Coaching points:
- move at least 1–2 metres in one direction and then quickly change direction;
- a passing fake should be convincing – move the arm with the ball out towards an imaginary teammate so that the defender can react to this and then correct to the actual direction of movement.

Common errors:
- attackers don't perform two fakes in a row;
- attackers drop the ball while performing one of these two moves.

drill 20 fakes in pairs

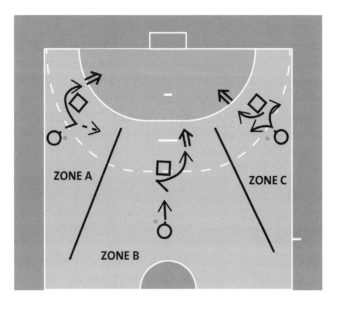

ZONE A

ZONE C

ZONE B

Objective: To repeat feints and changes of direction while working as attacker v defender.

Description: The attacker in zone A performs a change of direction combined with a passing feint. In zone B, the attacker performs a simple body feint and then goes past the defender to throw the ball at goal: fake to the left, then go right past the defender. Lastly, in zone C the attacker performs a double body feint: fake to the left, fake to the right and finally go left past the defender.

Coaching points:
- make a convincing move by moving 1–2 metres in the direction of the fake and then sprinting in the new direction;
- be strong with the ball during the change of direction, ideally holding it with both hands.

Common errors:
- attackers do not perform convincing moves;
- attackers run into the defenders;
- attackers drop the ball while performing these moves.

Throws at goal

The main aim of the game – scoring goals – is what all players like to do. This essential skill demands several techniques which are determined by the nature of the throw: stationary throw, e.g. the 7-metre throw; running throw, jumping throw and diving throw.

Player performing a jump throw

drill 21 the stationary throw at goal

Objective: To practise the stationary throw.

Description: The standing throw is used for the free throws, the 9-metre throws, the 7-metre throws and the side line throws. The body weight is on the opposite leg to the throwing arm. The leg is placed slightly forward, the body is relaxed and ready to execute a brief and strong move. The arm with the ball is drawn backward, the torso turned and the shoulder opposite to the throwing arm is facing towards the goal. The upper body executes a rotation that brings the shoulders level; at this point the ball is thrown powerfully at goal.

Coaching points:
- when throwing the ball, move the arm with the ball backwards and then powerfully bring it forwards;
- the shoulder opposite to the throwing arm should be facing towards the goal;
- rotate the upper body at the moment of the throw so the shoulders are on the same level.

Common errors:
- the arm with the ball is not moved backwards before the shot and there is no power in the throw;
- there is no upper body rotation.

drill 22 — the jump-in shot with side step or crossed-step take-off

Objective: To develop ability with more complex shots.

Description: This shot is similar to the previous one regarding the activity of the upper body. The difference is in the steps preceding the take-off: the side steps and the crossed-over steps are executed in three steps. The first step corresponds to the first move and it is executed with the leg opposite to the throwing arm. The second step corresponds to the moment of getting the legs closer; the third step is dedicated to the throw and it is executed during the second sidestep/crossed-over step.

Coaching points:
- the steps are executed with the feet completely off the floor for the efficiency of take-off;
- the take-off always starts with the opposite foot to the throwing arm – for the jump throw, the pivoting is done with the opposite foot to the throwing arm;
- the torso is not bent;
- the arm with the ball is over the shoulder;
- for the jump throw, the foot corresponding to the throwing arm is positioned behind.

Common errors:
- the feet are still on the floor when they should be in take-off;
- while setting up the throw, the player moves his arm close to the body and then to the back, instead of just taking it straight to the back;
- the hand is relaxed during the throw;
- the torso does not execute the turn-around correctly for precision, force and direction of the ball.

drill 23 | diving throw

Objective: To develop confidence and ability to perform a diving throw.

Description: One of the most spectacular throws in the game of handball, the diving throw, requires certain abilities from the attacker especially on the landing after releasing the ball. The diving throw is used for throws from the wing, at the edge of the semicircle. The player with the ball jumps up and, just before throwing the ball, twists laterally so that he is almost horizontal in the air. The hand that holds the ball is usually above his body. By performing this move, the shooter gets closer to the centre of the 6-metre semicircle and opens up his shooting angle. In order to be legal, the throw must be made before the player touches the floor.

Coaching points:
- the hand with the ball should be above the body;
- release the ball before landing.

Common errors:
- the player is touching the floor in landing before releasing the ball;
- the arm with the ball is being held under the body so there is not enough power in the shot.

drill 24 the goal

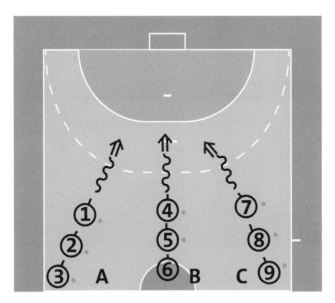

Objective: To learn how to throw the ball towards the goal.

Description: The players form three lines (A, B and C) about 11–12 metres in front of the goal. In turns, they all dribble once towards the goal and take a shot as a jump throw. After this shot, Player 1 will move to the back of line B; Player 4 will move from line B to C and so on – in this way they practise shooting from different positions.

Coaching points:
- jump powerfully upwards and forwards;
- aim for the corners of the goal – top left, top right, bottom left, bottom right;
- catch the ball with both hands at the end of the dribble before you take the shot.

Progression:
- introduce a goalkeeper;
- alternate the type of throw – jump throw, hip throw, lateral throw, etc;
- players could use side steps or crossed over steps.

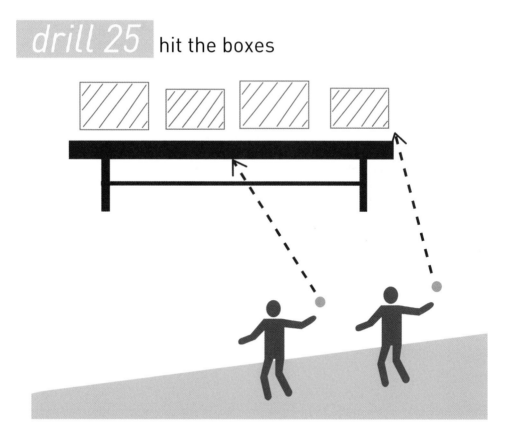

Objective: To improve throwing accuracy.

Description: Two (or more) players are lined up in front of a bench that has several boxes (or various objects) placed on it. At a signal, the players will throw the ball trying to hit the boxes on the bench. The winner will be the one who hits the most boxes.

Coaching points:
- send the ball powerfully and aim at the object;
- follow through after the shot.

Progression:
- increase the distance;
- add a dribble before the throw.

School of the ball – games, relays and drills

All the drills and exercises in this section can be grouped under the title of 'School of the ball'. School of the ball describes all the drills needed to acquire ball handling skills, and learn the fundamental techniques of this sport in an easy and fun manner. These are simple and stimulating drills and can be adapted depending on the main objectives of the lesson. Getting possession of the ball during the game can motivate the players, thus making them more determined to get involved in the activity and acquire a set of complex motor skills. These games and relays cover: getting used to the ball; assessing the distance to a teammate; adjusting the body position depending on the trajectory and speed of the ball; the ability to hold, catch and pass the ball to a teammate; developing attention skills, team spirit, motor memory, space awareness and ambidexterity.

drill 26 simple relay

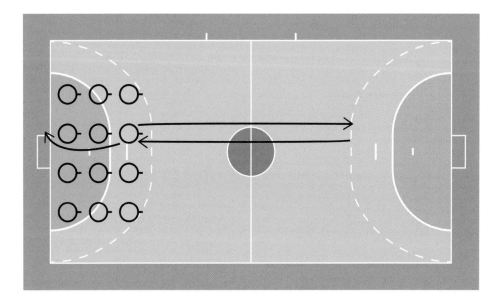

Objective: To improve movement on court and to work as a team.

Description: In groups of 3–4 players, positioned on a starting point: at a signal the first player races to a predetermined finish line (half way line, the other 6-metre semicircle, etc.). Once they touch that line, they run back to their team and the second player takes their turn.

Coaching points:
- use both arms when running;
- do not leave until your teammate has come back to the starting line.

Progression:
- running forwards to the finish line and running backwards from that line back to the starting point;
- run while carrying a handball.

drill 27 running by letters

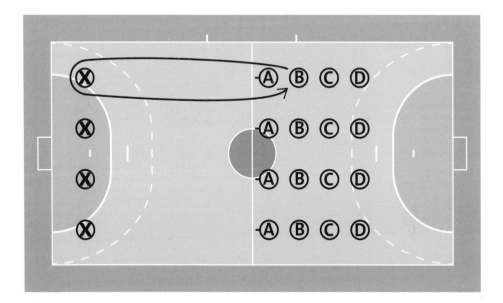

Objective: To improve attention and reaction time.

Description: Each player will be allocated a letter. When the coach calls a letter, the players allocated that letter will run a certain distance, determined beforehand, and then go back to the starting point. This can be performed as a competition, with each player who returns first receiving a point.

Coaching point: Pay attention to what letter is being called.

Progression:
- players run through cones placed on court at various intervals;
- players need to perform a specific action when they get to the finish point: star jump, push up, etc.

drill 28 'rats and rabbits'

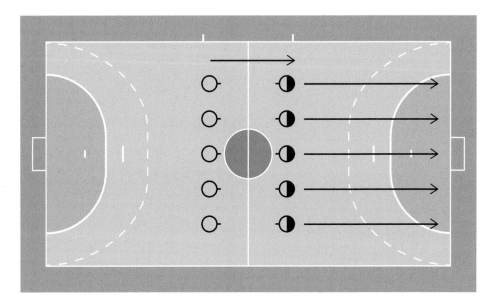

Objective: To improve reaction time and speed.

Description: Players are divided into two teams facing each other on either side of the halfway line. One team are the 'rats' and the other team are the 'rabbits'. When the coach says 'rats', the rats will have to chase and catch the rabbits up to an agreed line on the court, and vice versa.

Coaching points:
- do not push people when you tag them;
- run in a straight line to get the person in front of you rather than going across the court.

Progression:
- all players start from various positions: lying down, while doing push-ups, sit-ups, etc.;
- place balls between the two teams and the team that is chasing have to get possession of the ball and aim to touch the running players with the ball;
- signals or words other than those expected by the players can be used – 'radish', 'reds', or a clap of hands instead of whistle – to get players to pay attention and to focus on the commands;
- both teams run backwards or sideways.

drill 29 the ball on the bridge

Objective: To become familiar with the ball and to work together as a team.

Description: Players are divided into teams of 4–5 players. Each team lines up in single file with each player one arm's length away from the person in front. The first player in each team has a ball – they pass it over the head to the next player in the queue, and so on until the ball arrives at the last player who will take the ball to the front and will repeat the same action. When the player who was initially first gets back to the front of the queue that team has won.

Coaching points:
- do not throw the ball to the person who is behind you – you must pass it over the head;
- maintain the shape of your team as a single file formation at all times.

Common errors:
- players throw the ball to the next player in the queue instead of passing it;
- players do not maintain the distance required which makes passing the ball difficult.

drill 30 the ball through the tunnel

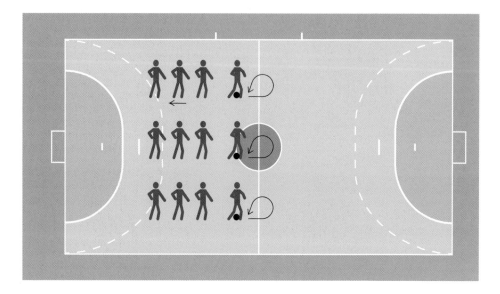

Objective: To be able to handle the ball and to work together as a team.

Description: Players are divided into teams in the same manner as in the previous drill. All of them need to stand with feet shoulder width apart, about one arms-length away from the person in front. The game starts at a signal – the first player rolls the ball through the legs of the team towards the last member. Once the ball arrives at the last player in the queue, it is picked up and run to the front of the queue before repeating the same action. When the player who was initially first gets back to the front of the queue, that team wins the race.

Coaching points:
- keep your feet wide apart;
- do not throw the ball – you have to roll it towards the back of your team.

Progression: Instead of rolling the ball on the floor the players are asked to hand it back between their legs to the person behind.

drill 31 relay with handballs

Objective: To become familiar with the ball; to improve speed while performing other actions.

Description: The players are divided into 2–4 rows behind the 9-metre semicircle. The first player in each team holds a handball with both hands. At a signal, they run, go around a cone placed 8–10 m away, and return to their team to hand over the ball to the next player and go to the back of the queue. The game ends when the first player is at the front of the queue again.

Coaching points:
- do not let the ball drop on the floor – always hold it with both hands;
- keep your head up when you run.

Progression: The instruction can be changed to: run and dribble the ball with the right hand all the way to the cone and back; same thing with the left hand; dribble with the right hand on the way to the cone and with the left hand on the way back.

drill 32 keep your court clean

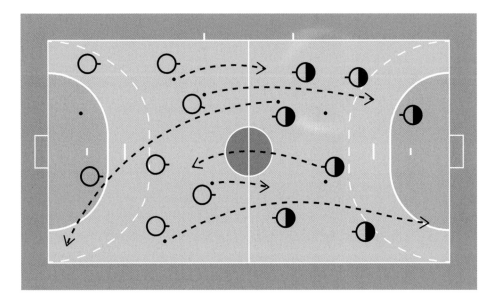

Objective: To work on throwing skills and to be aware of balls coming to own half from the opposite court.

Description: The players are divided into two teams, with the players spread out on their half of the court, and with 10–12 balls per team. Each team has the task of throwing the balls from its own half onto the half of the opposing team. While throwing the balls, all players attempt to collect the balls landing on their half as quickly as possible. When the whistle is blown the team with the fewest balls on its own court will be the winning team.

Coaching points:
- try to throw the ball into an area of the court containing no players;
- be aware of the balls being thrown by the other team players so that you do not get hit.

Common errors:
- players are rolling the balls and not throwing them onto the other court;
- players wait for the ball to come to them instead of going to get it;
- players throw the ball straight into an opposing player instead of throwing it into a space where no opposing players are.

drill 33 ball to the captain

Objective: To improve passing skills; to work on simple leadership skills.

Description: Players are divided into equal teams and lined up in a single file formation. One player in each team starts the game as captain – he will stand with a ball in his hands 4–5 metres in front of his team of 'soldiers'. At the starting signal, the captain passes the ball to the first soldier in the queue, who passes back to the captain and who will then join the back of the queue. The captain passes to the second player in the queue who will do the same, and so on until all the soldiers have been passed the ball. Then the next player from the queue will become captain, while the initial captain will join the group.

Coaching points:
- passes must be accurate;
- single file formation must be maintained throughout the game.

Progression: Various types of passes must be performed: chest pass, bounce pass, pronation pass.

drill 34 drill 34 zig-zag ball

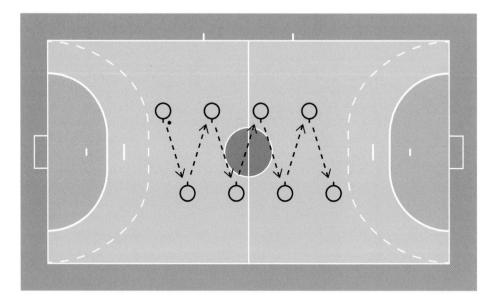

Objective: To improve passing accuracy.

Description: The players are placed in two rows, about 4 metres apart and with 2–3 metres between each player. One ball is used – it will be passed down the line from one row to another in a zigzag manner.

Coaching points:
- step into the pass;
- send a powerful pass, using a flat trajectory;
- have your hands ready to receive the pass (palms open, fingers spread out).

Progression: The same drill can be performed using two balls – one can be passed using a chest pass while the second ball is sent using a bounce pass.

drill 35 relay with dribbling

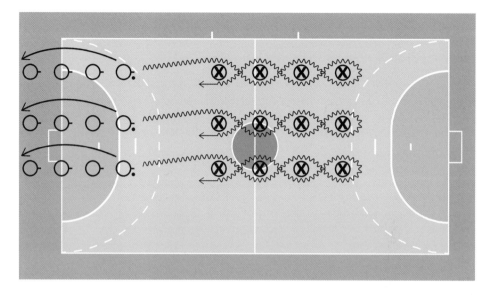

Objective: To improve dribbling skills, to improve speed and to work as a team.

Description: Teams are lined up in single file behind a start line, with cones placed 5-6 m away. The first player in each team has the ball. At the whistle, the first player starts dribbling the ball to the cone, around it and back before giving the ball to the next player, and then joins the back of the queue. The game ends when the first player gets back to the front and receives the ball. If any player drops the ball they must pick it up and carry on from that position.

Coaching points:
- keep your head up while dribbling;
- dribble the ball slightly to the side of your body so the ball does not run under your feet;
- avoid placing the palm under the ball.

Progression: same race and same set up but this time each player will dribble between the cones.

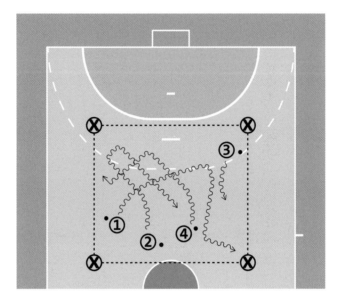

Objective: To improve dribbling skills.

Description: A rectangular space is coned out, where the players will execute dribbles in various directions and using both hands, without touching one another. Players must be on the move at all times.

Coaching point: The coach needs to instruct the players to keep their heads up and their eyes on the other players, not on the ball.

Progression: Dribble with the weaker hand.

relay combining dribbling, passing and catching

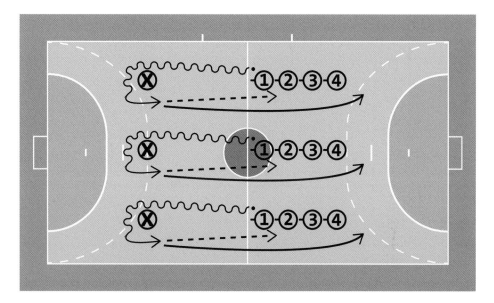

Objective: To improve the basic skills of dribbling and passing.

Description: Several teams are lined up behind the starting line, i.e. the half way line or one of the semicircles, with cones placed 5–6 m away. The first player in each row has a handball. At the whistle, he starts running and dribbling towards the cone, around it and then passes the ball to the next player; afterwards, he runs to join the back of the team. The game is won when the first player gets to the front of the group and receives the ball from the last player.

Coaching points:
- keep your head up while dribbling the ball;
- use both hands when dribbling between the cones;
- send accurate passes.

Progression: Use various types of passes.

drill 38 hit the tower with the ball

Objective: To develop quick thinking and teamwork; to improve accuracy of throws; to work on basic defending.

Description: The players are placed in a circle with one ball between them. In the middle of the circle is a chair (the tower) and a player stands near it, trying to defend it. The players in the circle pass the ball among themselves in order to distract the guardian of the tower and to create a favourable situation to hit the tower. When the tower is hit, the guardian switches places with the player who successfully threw. This drill requires players' cooperation and quick thinking, and attention to the location of the guardian, so that a quick pass is sent to the opposite side of the circle for a clean shot at the tower. Also, the defender has a chance to rehearse various defending moves in blocking the shots.

Coaching points:
- communicate and work together as a team;
- look to pass the ball quickly and accurately to your teammates;
- use various defending moves to protect the tower, e.g. block shots, move using side steps, etc.

Progression: The attacking team has only 5 passes to hit the tower.

drill 39 pig in the middle

Objective: To improve passing skills; to develop player ability to intercept the ball.

Description: In a limited space (3 x 3 metres square, or 4 x 4 metres square), two players move and pass the ball to each other. A defender attempts to intercept the ball. If the defending player manages to get possession of the ball, the losing attacker now becomes defender.

Coaching points:
- accuracy of passes is vital; pass and move all the time;
- as a defender be proactive and force the attackers to make a mistake.

Progression: Play as 3 attackers v 2 defenders.

the hen defends the chicks

Objective: To improve accuracy in passing the ball; to improve cooperation and working together as a team; to improve quick thinking and decision making.

Description: Players are divided into two teams of 6–7 players: Team A will form a circle, with Team B inside the circle in single file. The first player in Team B is the hen, the rest of Team B are the chicks. The players in Team B hold on to each other at hip level with the hen at the front of the line. Team A have a ball that they use to target the last chick. At the whistle, Team A pass the ball around so the ball is close to the end of Team B, exactly where the last chick is situated. The hen and the chicks need to move in such a manner that the hen will always be able to protect the chicks by blocking the shots or intercepting the passes. The chick that gets hit by the ball is out of the game. Change roles after 60 seconds. The team that hits the most chicks is the winner.

Coaching points:
- work together as a team in order to pass the ball quickly, or to defend the chicks;
- communicate with each other, especially the hen and the chicks.

Progression: Use only a particular type of pass, e.g. bounce pass, pronation pass, etc.

hit below the knee (defend and attack)

Objective: To rehearse the basic defending position.

Description: The players are grouped in pairs and they must try to touch their partner's foot below the knee with their open palm while making sure they do not get touched. Players can use their arms to protect their lower legs and can use fake moves to catch their partner off-guard for an easy hit. The coach needs to ask players to be sensible when attacking and defending. Each time a player hits below the knee a point is scored. The first player to score 10 points wins. All players need to be well spread out on the court.

Coaching points:
- be careful not to bang heads when attacking your opponent;
- keep moving using side steps, lateral moves, etc;
- bend your knees and maintain a low body position.

Progression: The game can be played for a specific duration, e.g. 30 seconds, 1 minute, etc.

drill 42 who keeps possession longest?

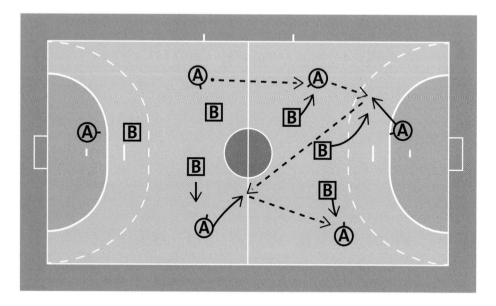

Objective: To improve passing and to work together as a team; to work on defending skills; to improve players' ability to intercept the ball.

Description: Two teams of equal numbers play against each other. Team A has possession while team B plays in defence. The aim of the game is for Team A to make 10 or 15 consecutive passes while Team B is trying to intercept the ball. There is no dribbling and no throws to goal – this is just a passing game. Depending on the number of players in each team, the game can be played on a half-court or full court. All rules regarding three steps, three seconds, side line boundaries of court and illegal fouls will apply.

Coaching points:
- pass and move at all times – move when you do not have the ball so that you can be free to receive the ball;
- communicate with each other;
- guard an opposite team player and put pressure on the ball by guarding it closely.

Progression: A specific type of pass must be used, e.g. chest pass, bounce pass, etc.

passing in a square

Objective: To develop passing and moving skills; to improve thinking and decision making skills.

Description: All players stand in a square. One player has the ball and starts the drill. He needs to pass to the first player from the queue that is on his right hand side and then he will follow his pass. The drill goes on with the ball moving along the square and players following their pass.

Coaching points:
- send an accurate pass to your partner's chest level;
- move the ball from the back to the front when you pass.

Progression:
- this drill can be performed with two balls being passed at the same time;
- ask players to pass to the right and then run and join the queue on the left – this enhances their thinking while passing the ball.

drill 44 passing in pairs on the move

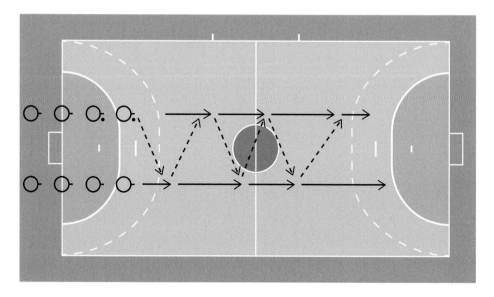

Objective: To improve passing skills; this drill could be used as a warming up exercise too.

Description: All players are grouped in pairs in front of one goal, just inside the 6-metre semicircle. At the start signal, the player with the ball passes it to his partner and then runs forward so that he can receive the ball from a different position on the court. They keep passing and running until they get to the other end of court. The second pair in the queue will wait for the pair in front of them to go over the half way line before they start their turn.

Coaching points:
- pass the ball slightly ahead of the moving player and not behind him;
- the ball must have a flat trajectory.

Progression: When the pair arrive at the other goal (around the 9-metre semicircle), one of them will take a shot.

drill 45 the colours

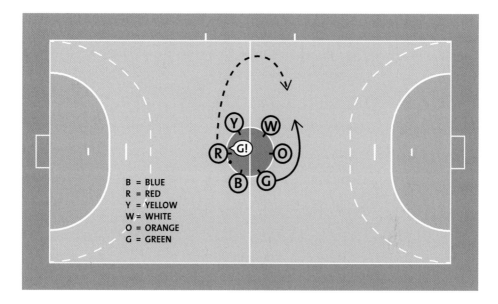

B = BLUE
R = RED
Y = YELLOW
W = WHITE
O = ORANGE
G = GREEN

Objective: To improve reaction time and quick thinking; to improve catching the ball under pressure.

Description: Players are divided into groups of 5–6 players and stand in a circle with one ball between them. Each player from the group picks a colour. The player with the ball throws it in the air and shouts a colour from the group. The player who hears his colour must catch the ball before it hits the ground. If he does, that player continues the game; if not, the game continues with the ball being thrown by the same player. The team that manages to resume the game more times than the other team will win.

Coaching points:
- catch the ball using both hands;
- keep an eye on the ball if your colour has been called.

Common errors:
- players do not have their hands ready to catch the ball;
- players do not pay attention to the colour being shouted and miss their turn.

drill 46 harvesting and seeding potatoes

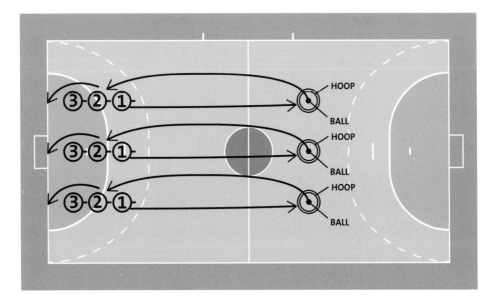

Objective: To become familiar with the handball and be able to handle it safely.

Description: Players are divided into 3–4 teams behind a line on the court, e.g. the 9-metre semicircle. Hoops are placed 10–15 metres from the first player in each team, with a handball in each hoop. At the whistle, the first player in each team must run to their hoop and 'harvest' the ball, (pick it up with both hands), and run back to his team to hand it to the next player. This player now has the task of 'seeding' the ball, (to run with it back to the hoop). He is not allowed to throw the ball – he has to place it carefully so it stays inside the hoop. The game is won when the last player in one team accomplishes the task.

Coaching points:
- do not throw the ball into the hoop;
- carry the ball using both hands.

Progression: Play with 2 hoops containing balls to each team. Players will follow the same pattern – run and harvest the balls, then bring them quickly back to the next teammate in the queue who will seed them.

drill 47 ball to the captain who is in goal

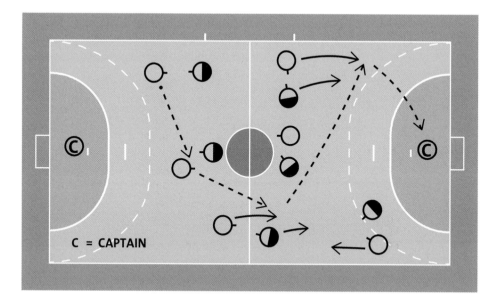

C = CAPTAIN

Objective: To improve passing and moving on court; to increase awareness of defenders.

Description: This game is played on the full court. Players are divided into two equal teams. Each team nominates a captain who is placed in the goal at the opposite end of the court. One team has possession of the ball and starts the game. The aim is to get as close as possible to the captain by passing the ball and by running and moving on the court, so that they eventually can pass the ball safely to him. If they manage to do this, they score a point. As a general rule, the ball cannot be thrown from the players' own half of the court to the opposite goal area – the ball has to be passed between the players. The defending team will try to prevent the other team from scoring. After a few points have been scored, a new captain goes in goal.

Coaching points:
- pass and move into space;
- communicate with your teammates;
- defending players can use a 'man to man' marking tactic.

Progression: The ball has to be touched by all members of the team before a goal can be scored. A time limit can be set for the team that has possession of the ball, e.g. 1 minute, 30 seconds or 20 seconds to score a goal.

drill 48 2 players pass 2 balls

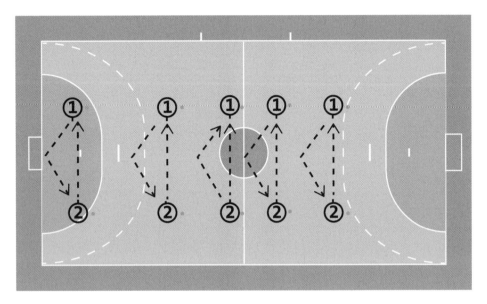

Objective: To practise passing and catching the ball.

Description: Players work in pairs, each player has a ball and they are spread all over the court at a distance of 5–6 metres from one another. Player 1 will send a chest pass to Player 2, while Player 2 will throw a bounce pass to Player 1 at the same time. After a certain number of passes they need to swap the type of pass: Player 1 will bounce pass, while Player 2 will chest pass.

Coaching points:
- catch the ball with two hands;
- send accurate passes, powerful enough to get to your teammate;
- communicate with your partner when you change the type of pass.

Progression:
- change the type of pass, for example send an overhead pass instead of a chest pass;
- the players could jog while they pass from one end of the court to the other.

drill 49 pass in triangles

Objective: To practise passing and catching the ball.

Description: Players stand in groups of three in a triangle. The drill starts with Players A and B with a ball each, while Player C is the passing player. Player A will pass to Player C who will return to Player A; then Player B will pass to Player C who will pass back to Player B. The drill continues for a certain number of passes, or a certain amount of time – 30 seconds or 1 minute for example. Afterwards, Player A can be the passing player who will pass the ball back to Player B and Player C.

Coaching points:
- always catch the ball with both hands;
- send a flat, accurate pass to your teammate so that it gets to the receiver at chest level.

Progression:
- change the type of pass;
- increase the distance between the players.

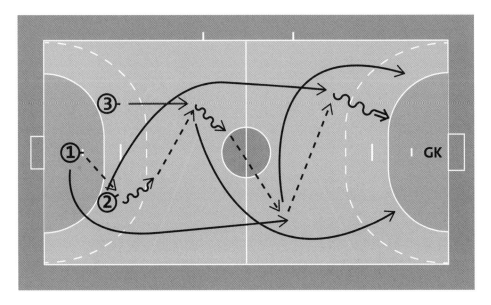

Objective: To practise passing on the move; to practise occupying a space on court.

Description: Players are in groups of three and each group has one ball. At the starting signal, Player 1 passes to Player 2 and will follow his pass by going towards the outside of court and the opposite goal. When Player 2 gets the ball, he changes direction and dribbles once towards the middle of the court, being ready to pass to the third player in the group who will repeat the same move. When close to the opposite goal, the player who has the ball can shoot. The drill demands accurate passing and develops the ability of players to pass and anticipate other's people moves while running.

Coaching points:
- pass and follow your pass around the outside of the player you passed to;
- run towards the other goal if you do not have the ball and always aim to be ahead of the ball;
- each player runs inside their channel – once a player has left his channel, someone else needs to fill that space.

Progression:
- perform the drill without dribbling;
- a defender can play on the 6-metre semicircle where players will shoot from.

drill 51 half court passing

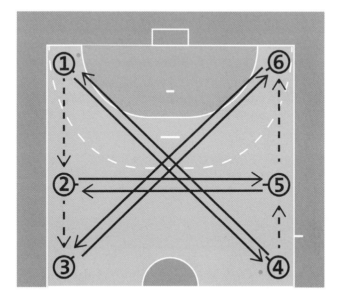

Objective: To improve passing and catching; to develop awareness of on-coming passes and movement without the ball.

Description: Players are lined up all facing into the court. Players 1 and 4 have a ball each and they start the drill by passing the ball to the player who is on their right hand side. Once the ball is passed, each player must run across or diagonally to the other side of court.

Coaching points:
- make flat, crisp and accurate passes;
- call the name of the person receiving the pass;
- pass to the right and run to the opposite sideline.

Progression:
- perform the drill on the full court;
- players run sideways when they go to the next spot.

drill 52 bench dribble drill

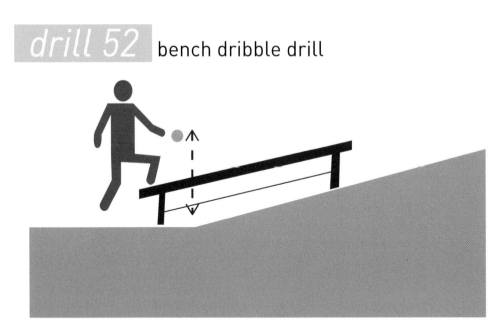

Objective: To improve coordination and dribbling skills.

Description: Note: before the drill starts the coach needs to check if the bench is stable. Each player has a ball and starts the drill next to the bench. At the starting signal, Player 1 will start dribbling the ball with his right hand while stepping along the bench with his right foot (his left foot will be on the floor). He continues to dribble and to step until he gets to the end of the bench. Player 1 then goes to the back of the queue and Player 2 will start.

Coaching points:
- do not slap the ball – keep it under control;
- make sure you step properly onto the bench;
- try to coordinate your dribbling arm with your feet/legs.

Progression:
- dribble with the left hand and step onto the bench with your left foot;
- dribble the ball on the bench while you walk next to it;
- add another action at the end (pass, another dribble, a shot at goal, etc).

drill 53 jumps over a bench

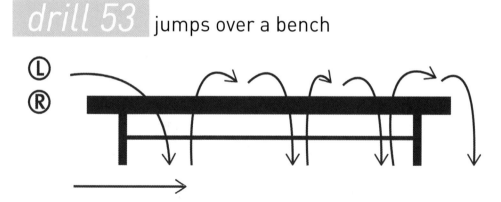

Objective: To develop jumping ability; to improve agility and coordination.

Description: One player at a time performs consecutive jumps over the bench from one end to the other without touching the bench. As a safety precaution the next player in the queue will start jumping only when the player in front of him has finished. The coach must ensure the bench is stable before starting the drill.

Coaching points:
- be on your toes;
- use your arms when jumping and when landing;
- on landing jump immediately onto the other side.

Progression: At the end you can receive a ball and dribble towards the goal and shoot.

Ivano Balic (right) of Madrid challenges for the ball with Denis Spoljaric (left) of Berlin during the HBL Champions League in Berlin, Germany (photo by Luis Ramirez/ LatinContent/Getty Images)

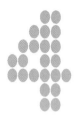

TACTICS IN HANDBALL

Sport tactics consist of the organisation and coordination of players' actions in order to achieve success, usually obtained by the conscious use – within the limits of rules and fair play spirit – of the most effective actions, by maximising the players' qualities and by exploiting the weak points of the opponents. Tactical training does not receive enough attention during the instruction of children or beginners mainly because the main objective of training at that stage is focused on the 'school of the ball', on the games, relays and drills meant to introduce them gradually to the real handball game.

In terms of tactical preparation, children and beginners must acquire all the tactical aspects related to the executions of technical elements, and the basic notions of collective tactics. The learning of tactics should synchronise with the level reached by the children in technical instruction. The tactical knowledge is acquired only if the technique learnt is properly executed.

Analysis of players' activity during matches shows that the two components, technical and tactical, are inseparable and that they constitute a single unit most of the time. The technical and tactical actions differ widely from one stage of coaching to another and even from one game situation to another. This means that technical and tactical training should be delivered globally alongside the analytical aspect.

This element demands that all players must be able to play any position, except that of the goalkeeper, to a basic level. Once they have learned this, they will continue to improve their basic technique and start specialising on position lines (6-metre and 9-metre). This specialisation of positions will depend on the somatotype of children and on their physical qualities, strength, speed, power, etc., as shown below.

Even after this stage is complete, the improvement of basic techniques and tactics must continue and should remain a priority in children's instruction. The player now must now develop the ability to apply highly skilled execution in games.

A handball team's tactics are team strategies that focus on the faults of the opposing team and create advantages for their own team. Obvious faults in the training of opponents are counterweighted by the best developed components within the training of their own players. If a team is very well trained physically, technically, theoretically, then tactics are crucial in determining the winner.

The tactics adopted by a team can be characterised by two main elements: accessibility – tactics should correspond to the technical level, to the physical and mental abilities of the players; and flexibility – players should be able to adjust to the problematic situations of the game, to act creatively and responsibly to advantage their own team.

Game tactics consist of individual tactical actions with and without the ball; collective tactical actions of collaboration between two or more players; team-specific collective tactical actions.

Individual tactical actions in attack

Individual tactics in attack include getting open, drawing in a defender, getting past the opponent, looking for a chance to score, anticipating the actions of the opponent and limiting long passes. Every court player has several possible individual tactics including moving in the free space; effective, timely passes; monitoring the reactions of the opponent and drawing attention to his own actions; choosing a move that facilitates the action of the teammate; choosing the finalising action for the offence; choosing the trajectory of the shots; analysing specific situations (such as goalkeeper position/placement in goal) and determining the way the offence will be run.

The modern handball game is characterised by the speed of the attack. The purpose of the attackers is twofold: firstly, to defeat the defenders through surprising actions; secondly, to move effectively on court to handle the ball, and do this by collaborating with each other.

Passing the ball is the simplest way to disrupt the opponents' defence system. Through repeated passes corridors and spaces are created in the defensive system. These corridors enable penetrations, long throws at goal or even the involvement of the pivot around the semicircle area. The pass also has to be powerful enough to stop defenders intercepting the ball. Diagonal, long passes over several defence zones are usually not effective. A long throw should be used only if a corridor was created in the opposing defence system. Transmitting the ball with high speed, without holding it too much and without dribbling, brings more advantages to the team than disadvantages. Excessive dribbling slows down the passing speed and thus the quality of the game. In the direct fight with a defender, protection of the ball will be paramount and this forces the attacker to put his body between the ball and the opponent.

The players who throw the ball from the wing position must widen the throwing angle to give them the chance to beat the goalkeeper. They will alternate powerful and lob shots over the goalkeeper, depending on their position.

drill 54 throw the ball from the wing

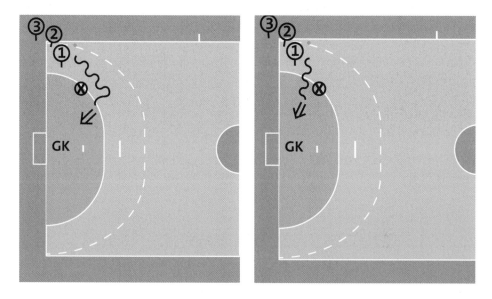

Objective: To develop skill in approaching a shot from the wing.

Description: Players are lined up in single file on the corner of the court with a cone in front of them. They have a ball each. Taking in turns, they dribble only once towards the cone, around it and throw the ball at goal to try to score.

Coaching points:
- jump high and forward towards the goal;
- release the ball before landing inside the 6-metre semicircle.

Common errors:
- the jump is not powerful enough;
- players land in the 6-metre area before they release the ball;
- there is not enough power in the shot.

Progression:
- a passive defender could be placed on the semicircle instead of the cone;
- the attackers are sent inside the cone as opposed to outside of it.

drill 55 getting open in a 1 v 1 situation

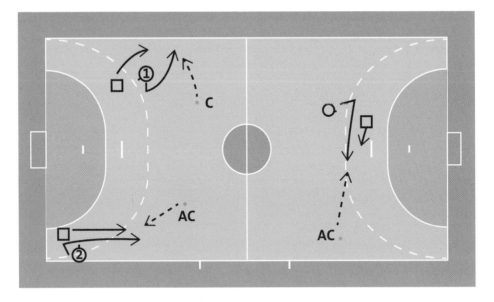

Objective: To practise movement to receive the ball.

Description: Players work in pairs; one player is attacker and one is defender. The coach will start with the ball. The attacker will make a fake move and change direction, trying to get open so that he can receive the ball from the coach. The defender will try to guard so the attacker cannot receive the ball – he can deny the pass or even intercept it.

Coaching points:
- make a convincing move of 2–3 metres away from the ball before you sprint in a new direction closer to the ball;
- have your arms ready to receive the pass;
- you can use multiple fakes before you actually get open to receive the ball.

Common errors:
- the fake move is not convincing enough to beat the defender;
- the attacker pushes the defender when he is changing direction.

Progression:
- this drill can be implemented in various parts of the court: central; on the wing; etc.
- it can be played as a 2 v 2 drill as well.

Players' qualities and roles depending on position

The exact position of attacking players on court is determined by the playing system used by the team, as well as by the defensive system used by the opponents. By training the attackers in position, they become more efficient, though nowadays they must be able to play in all positions. Deciding where to put your players must take into account the demands of the position and the physical, technical and tactical qualities of the attackers.

The wings are usually quick, and used as the main players in a fast break. They play at the sides of the court and at the corners, to weaken the opposing defence and to enlarge the penetrating spaces through the defenders – the concept of wide spacing is very important here. Their specific ability is scoring from narrow angles – see below – and they have the throwing skills to enlarge these angles.

The backs are tall, strong players, with good individual catching, passing and long throw skills – see page 88, top. In certain systems of play, they coordinate the team's attack. Through strong and long throws, they draw in the defenders and they create penetration or space for action for the pivots. They must know all the methods of passing to and involving the pivots – even the most subtle ones – and use them, but only when the tactics allows and when they can surprise the defence. They ensure the defensive balance is maintained and they are the first players who get back in defence in order to stop the opponents' fast break if the ball was lost during the attack.

Wing player trying to score from a narrow angle

The centre back, or playmaker, must have the skills to coordinate the specific actions of the team; he must have court and space awareness and he should master all types of passing, getting past the opponents, involving the pivots, throwing to goal – see above. He is usually one of the most experienced players on the team. Given his central position on the court, he has the task of passing the balls to the wings, to the backs and to the pivot.

The pivots, or circle runners, are the players who work on the 6-metre line. Two attacking systems require their actions: 5+1 and 4+2. They are strong players and their physical force is necessary in the close fight with the defenders on the semicircle. They are players with good motor skills, with speed of reaction and coordination. They are highly skilled, because they must handle the ball under very difficult circumstances and they must fight closely against the opponents.

Rebounding the ball after a missed shot is another tactic. This is effective in 7-metre throws, in particular when the ball saved by the goalkeeper or after hitting the post comes back into the playing area. Similarly, after the ball has been blocked by the defenders, the attackers need to be alert and get possession back by getting the rebound.

Team tactics in attack

The team attacking play – just like the defensive play – involves setting a well-determined tempo, and it focuses on surprising the opposing defence through carefully selected tactics, and actions designed to create scoring opportunities. The team attacking play can be divided into certain stages: the first phase which includes the fast break and the extended fast break; the second phase of the attack; the third phase of the attack and lastly when a certain attacking system is chosen. A brief overview of each phase is provided below.

The first phase of the attack – the fast break – involves creating a rapid scoring opportunity by using a few quick and very precise passes, and requires attention to the opponents' wings and pivot in particular. The fast break can be started by forcing the opponents to make a mistake and thus obtaining possession of the ball. Once possession is gained, the wings and the pivot from the team that now is on offence will distance themselves from the new defenders and will try to occupy the spaces that are left open. The running paths of those who execute the fast break will depend on the defenders' positions and the main aim is to create a situation where there are three or four attackers against fewer defenders. Players must ensure they are playing in position to avoid an inbalance in this system.

The fast break involves certain technical and tactical elements performed by 1–2 players:

- rapid and convenient, anticipated start;
- speed running;
- release of the ball by the goalkeeper or by an intermediary player;
- catching the ball coming from behind, at full speed;
- passes while running at full speed: sideward; diagonally across the court – to the front or to the back;
- direct outdistancing for opponent;
- a simple and/or multiple dribble in a straight line or with a change of direction;
- throw to goal, jumping throw or running throw, or even a hop throw to goal over the opposite goalkeeper.

Generally, the fast break leads to 18–25% of all the goals scored.

The extended fast break is a continuation of the initial fast break and involves some of the technical and tactical elements: passes between 2–3 running players; changes in direction and penetration through the defenders; outdistancing; involving the line players; long throws, such as running, leg switching, sidestepping, jumping.

The second phase of the attack must be carried out systematically, by determining precise player–ball paths with 3–5 options practised beforehand by the players and applied to the game.

The fast break, the second phase and the selection of a system of attack (5:1 or 4:2) must be performed as quickly as possible from the moment of possession so that it surprises the defence. Then, the attack must continue until the chance to throw to the goal arises.

fast break with two players

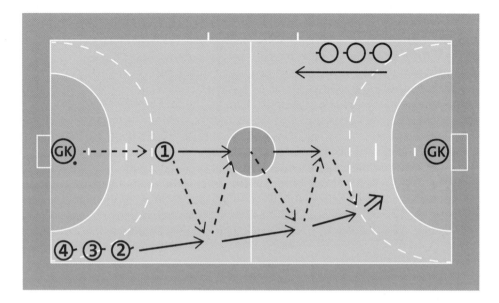

Objective: To practise the fast break action.

Description: Groups of players are placed on the wing position at each end of the court with one goalkeeper in each goal and one player in front of the 9-metre semicircle. The goalkeeper at one end starts the drill and passes the ball to Player 1 who then passes to Player 2. Players 1 and 2 continue to pass the ball between themselves moving towards the opposite goal – they need to keep running forward and to turn their upper body towards the sender of the pass each time when they receive the ball. Once they are close enough to the 6-metre semicircle, the ball is passed to the opposite goalkeeper and they join the back of the opposite team.

Common errors:
- players do not send accurate passes to each other when they perform the drill;
- players jog slowly instead of running.

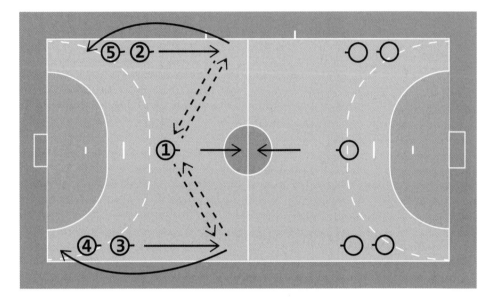

Objective: To rehearse the fast break action.

Description: Players are placed alongside each half of the court. Player 1, the centre back, starts the drill by passing either right or left – let's suppose the pass is to Player 2 who is running towards the half way line in order to receive. Player 2 passes back to the centre back who now passes onto the opposite side to player 3 who does the same – run, receive and pass back. After passing back to Player 1, the players on the wing jog back to join the back of the queue. The drill has to be done continuously with players timing their run depending on where the ball is.

Common errors:
- players do not time their run correctly;
- passes are not accurate.

drill 58 — fast break initiated by the goalkeeper

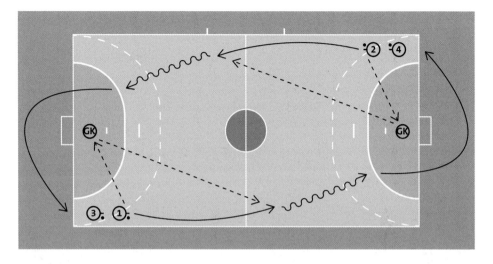

Objective: To learn the fast break initiated by the goalkeeper.

Description: A goalkeeper stands in each goal with all other players queuing to one side of goal at each end of the court. Player 1, on the wing, passes to the goalkeeper, runs on a fast break, receives the ball just over the half way line and then passes to the goalkeeper who is at the other goal; simultaneously player 2 performs the same move on the opposite wing.

Progression: Player 1 can finish his action with a shot at goal, instead of a pass.

2 v 1 fast break initiated by the goalkeeper

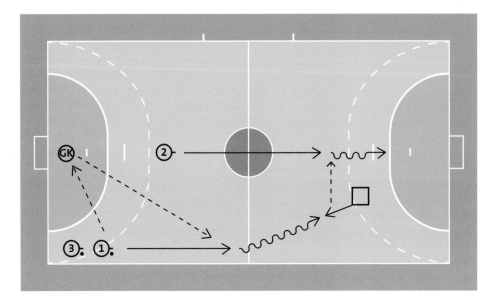

Objective: To rehearse the fast break action.

Description: Players are lined up on the wing, at one end of the court. A defender is placed at the opposite end on the 9-metre semicircle. Player 1 will start the drill together with Player 2, who is situated in the central area of the same half of the court as Player 1, in front of the 9-metre semicircle. Player 1 will pass the ball to the goalkeeper. After receiving the ball back from the goalkeeper, Player 1 will start the fast break by dribbling the ball towards the opposite goal. The defender at that end of the court will step towards Player 1, trying to stop the ball; this is when Player 1 will pass to Player 2 who is coming to support the attack. Player 2 will finish the fast break with a shot at goal.

Progression: This drill can also be used to practise the extended fast break.

drill 60
fast break with crossover between attackers

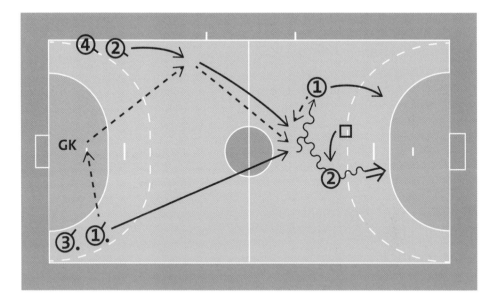

Objective: To practise the fast break with two players.

Description: All players are equally distributed on both wings at one end of the court. Player 1 starts the drill by passing to the goalkeeper. The goalkeeper then passes to Player 2 on the left wing who starts running on a fast break. After his pass, Player 1 sprints towards the central circle of the court where he receives from Player 2. From here, they switch sides and they play 2 v 1 against the defender who is waiting on the 9-metre semicircle. They finish with a throw to goal.

Common errors:
- players 1 and 2 run into each other when they attempt to switch sides;
- players do not send accurate passes.

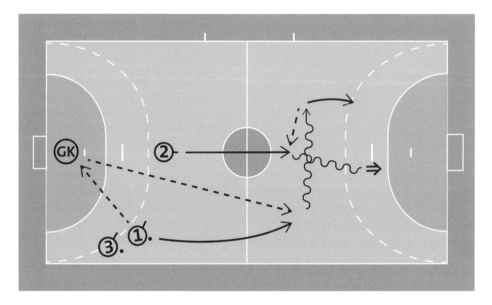

drill 61 the extended fast break

Objective: To practise the extended fast break.

Description: Players form one queue on the wing at one end of the court. A centre back player is situated in front of the 9-metre semicircle, while a defender is waiting at the other end of court. Player 1 starts the drill by passing the ball to the goalkeeper and then sprints on a fast break. Player 1 receives somewhere in the opposite court and dribbles across the court so that the defender comes to stop him. This is when Player 1 passes the ball to Player 2 who is trailing behind – they now switch places and Player 2 will finish with a throw to goal.

Common errors:
- players do not synchronise their switch and they bump into each other;
- players fail to send accurate passes.

The third phase of attack – of distributing the attacking players, of organising and reorganising the play (the offence) – sees an increase in game speed and permanent pressure on the opponents' defence.

The main aim of the attack is now to eliminate the stationary moments that determine the passive attack. The actions must be parallel with the goal and be offensive in nature, to use the whole playing space. The attack must switch between passing directly from an action of threatening the goal to an apparent scoring intention; the rhythm variations during this phase will help the element of surprise required to achieve a throw to goal.

The fourth phase of attack must be carefully organised; all players must be disciplined and they need to use their initiative and creativity in the last moments of the offence. This fourth phase involves shifting, tactical combinations and tactical schemes – the attackers will focus on outnumbering the opponents which will determine the outdistancing of a teammate off the direct marking of a defender. Thus, the last moment of offence becomes much easier, compared with the situation where an attacker has to fight in a one-on-one situation or even two-on-one with a defender. At this moment, players' focus should be on the following aspects:

- getting past the opponent in a 1:1 situation;
- collaboration between two attackers as a basic tactic, in which screening, getting out of the screen, the wall, the one-two, and the cross over, represent fundamental technical and tactical means;
- the play without the ball, which uses the spaces left by advanced defences, but also overtaking defenders to maintain the 2:2 and 1:1 situations.

drill 62 one-two, give and go

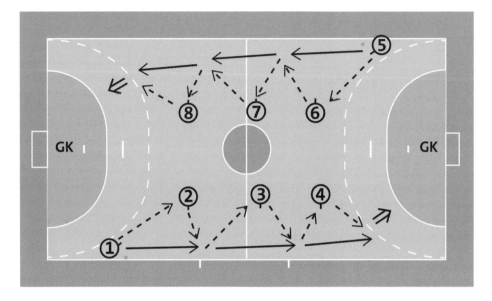

Objective: To practise the one-two (give and go) combination.

Description: Players are placed around the court. Players 1 and 5 have a ball each while Players 2, 3, 4, 6, 7 and 8 are static passing players. Player 1 passes the ball to Player 2 and immediately after the pass moves towards the opposite goal. After receiving the ball back from Player 2, it is then passed to Player 3 and performs a similar move – pass and cut to receive the ball back. After receiving from Player 4, Player 1 is now close to the 9-metre semicircle and he will take a shot at the goal. On the other side of the court, Player 5 will do exactly the same: pass and receive alternatively from Players 6, 7 and 8 and will finalise his actions with a shot at goal.

Coaching points:
- pass and cut, run towards the opposite goal, as soon as you release the ball;
- always catch the ball with both hands.

Progression:
- a bounce pass could be used;
- Player 1 can perform a change of direction fake after moving forward to receive from passing players.

drill 63 1 v 1 play

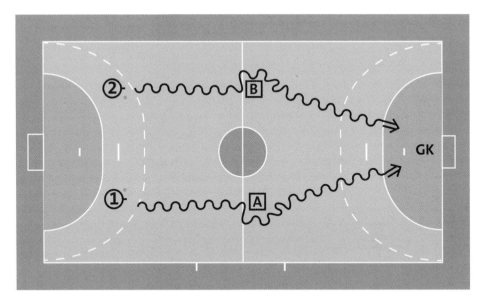

Objective: To practise playing 1 v 1.

Description: Two players, A and B, are defenders and they play on the half way line – they start as passive and then semi-active defenders, but they have to stay more or less on this line. Players 1 and 2 are attackers and have a ball each. Player 1 will dribble the ball towards Defender A and will make a change of direction when he is in front of the defender; then Player 1 will continue to dribble towards the goal and will take a shot. Similarly, Player 2 will do the same on the other side of the court, playing 1 v 1 against Defender B.

Coaching points:
- avoid catching the ball in both hands when in front of the defender;
- do not run into the defender – try to go past him.

Progression:
- defenders become active, but they stay on the half way line;
- defenders could be moved close to the goal, on the 9-metre semicircle.

screen and roll out of the screen

Objective: To practise the screen action.

Description: Players work in groups of 3: Players 1 and 2 are attackers while Player A is a defender, initially passive. Player 1 passes the ball to Player 2 and then he goes across to Defender A to set a screen on him. Player 2 will now dribble the ball past both teammate 1 and defender A in an attempt to throw to the goal. While Player 2 goes towards the goal, Player 1 will roll off the screen and have his hands ready in case he needs to receive the ball.

Coaching points:
- set a good screen with both feet on the ground and with your shoulders perpendicular to the defender's shoulder line;
- do not use your arms to push the defender or to embrace him;
- roll off the screen (when the teammate passes by) and have your arms ready to receive the ball.

Progression:
- Player 2 will now pass the ball to Player 1 who comes off the screen;
- defender becomes semi-active and then active;
- Attacker 1 will set a screen with his back at the Defender A (so will already be ready to receive the ball).

An attack with one or two pivots must be adapted to the actions of the defence. Unlike the defensive phase, the attack has the advantage of having ball possession and the possibility of taking some great moves in order to score. The defence aims to get possession of the ball through concrete defensive actions; this is followed by an organized attacking passage. As for the attack, every player must occupy his position without interrupting the movement of the ball. The construction of the attack for the final throw is based on tactical combinations and individual tactical actions. This final throw of the attack represents the climax of the actions made to score a point.

The fourth phase of the attack must be dynamic; with high-speed technical moves, in the action zones of each position, by passing from one wing to another, by fake throws, by getting past the opponents, or by using tactical combinations.

Success is related to the coordination of the individual players, as well as basic tactical means, in various forms and systems of attack. The defence can be efficient because all six defenders can cover the 6-metre line, the surface of the goal.

drill 65 five attackers v four defenders

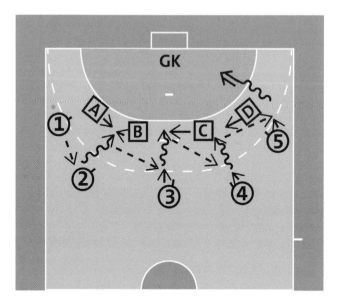

Objective: To learn how to attack with an extra player.

Description: Five attackers are placed on the 9-metre semicircle, while four defenders are placed on the 6-metre semicircle. Player 1 starts the drill by passing to Player 2 who will attack the space between the Defenders A and B. When B is closing down this space, Attacker 2 passes to 3 who will do the same – attack the space between Defenders B and C and so on until the ball arrives at Attacker 5 who will eventually have no defender in front of him. Player 5 will throw to goal unguarded from the wing area.

Coaching points:
- attack the gap between defenders and quickly pass the ball to the closest attacking teammate;
- pass the ball early and do not allow the defender to intercept it.

Progression:
- attacker 5 can return the ball from the right wing to the left wing player following a similar pattern of play;
- this drill can also be performed as 6 attackers v 5 defenders.

drill 66 — cooperation between wings and backs

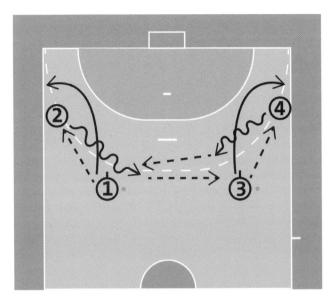

Objective: To practise passing between wings and backs.

Description: Players are in groups of four: two on the wing and two playing the back positions. Player 1 starts the drill by passing the ball to the wing Player 2. After the pass, Player 1 cuts towards the semicircle and then goes behind Player 2, who starts dribbling the ball towards the middle of the court. When he arrives at the left back position, he passes the ball to Player 3, who waits there. Player 3 will do the same as Player 1: pass the ball to Player 4, then go to the right wing. Player 4 will dribble the ball towards the middle of the court and when he gets to the right back spot he passes to Player 2, waiting at the left back position. They continue to pass and exchange places.

Coaching points:
- pass and move to the wing all the time when you are in the back player spot;
- accuracy of passes is important for the success of the drill.

Progression:
- after 5–6 passes players can take it in turns to throw the ball to the goal;
- passive defenders can be introduced who then become active.

drill 67
3 attackers v 2 defenders, with throw to goal from the central area

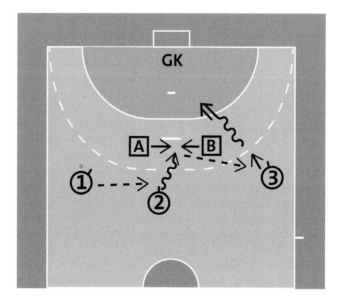

Objective: To practise attacking in a 3 v 2 situation.

Description: Attacker 1 starts the drill by passing the ball to Player 2. Player 2 will attack the space between the defenders A and B and Defender B will close this space down. Player 2 passes the ball to Player 3 who will dribble just once and then take the shot.

Coaching points:
- attack the space between two defenders;
- use passing fakes, change of direction fakes, etc.

Progression: Player 3 can reverse the ball to Player 2 who will send it to Player 1, and in this way Player 1 will take the shot.

The playing system is determined by the specific positioning of the offensive players when attacking the opposing goal. Regardless of the playing system used by the team, the basic principles and rules are always applicable.

The system of attack with one pivot

The attacking team uses a player as pivot at the 6-metre line – also called a circle runner. Another five players form a horseshoe shape outside the 9-metre line – see below. This system is useful when the aim is to get possession of the ball. The team sometimes has to apply this tactic towards the end of games, but it is also useful when the team leads by a few goals and wants to maintain the difference. Positioning or shifting the pivot must be in agreement with the direction of passing the ball.

Attacking system with one pivot (5:1)

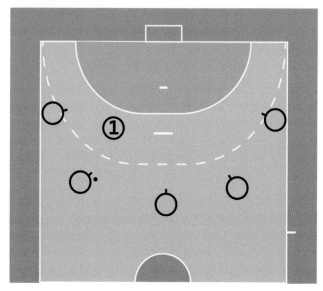

The system of attack with two pivots

The team places two pivots at the 6-metre line. This system is effective if the backs are good distance shooters and if the wings have a good technique, which helps them get past their opponents.

Both systems described above can be changed during play:

- one option is to transform it from 3+3 – when the opposing semicircle is overloaded for a short period – into 2+4, depending on the player who becomes the second pivot;
- another solution is to switch it from 2+4 into 3+3 attacking system, depending on the player who becomes the third 9-metre pivot;
- try with simulated (fake) transformations.

Attacking system with 2 pivots

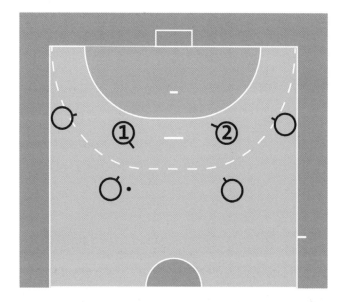

As mentioned before, attackers can collaborate with each other – some simple combinations are executed through passes among the players placed in certain positions:

- passes between the back and the wing, followed by throw to goal;
- passes between the right and the left back;
- passes over the semicircle between the two wings;
- passes between the wing, the play coordinator and the pivot;
- passes received by the pivot from the wings.

Other moves between two or three players specific to attacking play include:

The crossover is an attack-specific tactical action, executed by two or three players, in order to create an optimum distance for a throw to goal for one of them. For instance, the centre back penetrates toward the goal, passes to the left or right back and continues his penetration to the 6-metre line, in order to set a screen on a defender. The back receives the ball and throws to goal over the wall created by the centre back and by the pivot. If he is interrupted in his penetration toward the goal by the defenders, he can involve the pivot or he can pass to the other back who gets into the open space.

The wall is a collective tactical action that aims to facilitate a jump throw to goal from a distance, over the defenders. It is used to assist the 9-metre free throws for a jump shot following a pass. Two, three and sometimes more attackers form a wall in the free-throw area in front of the attacker who will execute a jump throw.

The **screen** is used with the intention to help a teammate who is being guarded closely man-to-man by an opponent, to get open and to facilitate throws to goal from distance over the defenders. For example: an opponent guards the left back man-to-man all over the court. In order to get open, the left back can use all the individual tactical means: starts, feints, changes in direction and of rhythm, etc. A teammate who sets a screen on the left back's direct defender can help him to get open so that he will throw to goal.

The screen

Similarly, other forms of screens can be used: a player with the ball sets a screen to a teammate without the ball; also, a player without the ball sets a screen to the man without the ball, so that he can get to open space. The screen can also have the purpose of creating a corridor in order to facilitate throws to goal from a distance.

The screen and getting out of the screen are shown below:

Attacking player setting a screen and getting out of the screen

Attacking player ready to receive the ball after getting out of the screen

One of the most desired attacking situations happens when attackers outnumber defenders – this usually occurs when the players start attacking early, for instance in fast breaks or in the second attack phase.

The 2:1 situation. If the wings start a fast break, they can outnumber the opponents as they could face a single defender, and this means they will try to score.

The 3:1 situation. It is important for the players to act as a triangle in order to minimise any chance for the defender to intercept the ball.

The 4:2 situation. In such situations, one or two players should sprint along the court; if they are not followed by defenders, they can receive a longitudinal pass and they can score.

The 4:3 situation. This is solved by wide attacking actions combined with the penetration of a player at the 6-metre line. Through effective and rapid passes, crossovers and getting open, the ball must get to the open player, who will score.

Tactical combinations for positional throws

a) Combinations for the 9-metre free throw. The attacking team forms a wall in front of the shooter. The players who do not form the wall must position themselves far from one another in order to prevent the opponents from focusing too much on the exact position of the free throw.

b) Tactical combinations for the throw-ins. For the success of such tactical combinations, a good technical and tactical training is required. The player who executes the throw-in passes to the pivot, situated on the semicircle, by using a powerful pass or a bounce pass. Another version successfully used for the throw-ins is based on a lob pass over the semicircle to a player who jumps out of the goal area, catches the ball in the air and immediately throws to goal.

c) Position of the attackers for the 7-metre throws. The attackers will be divided and placed on the court as follows: a player will execute the 7-metre throw (Player 1 in the figure below); three players (2, 3 and 4) will be placed on the 9-metre line, in order to rebound the balls that bounce back from the post or are saved by the goalkeeper; two players (5 and 6) move back to the centre in order to ensure the defensive balance.

Position of attackers for the 7 metre throw

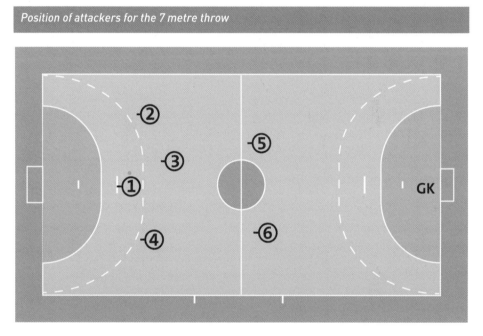

Attacking play in special situations

a) The attack with five players. A team may only have five players for a short period, following a suspension, so they will have to change tactics. The play is based on effectively shifting the ball and the players, with throws performed in clear scoring situations only. In such cases, it is not acceptable to throw to goal without any tactical justification or from bad positions.

b) The attack against five defenders. There are situations when a full team has a hard time scoring against a team without all the members, also following the suspension of a player. The attacking team should use the attack with 2 pivots and four players in the free-throw area; the wings are situated to the sides of the playing court in order to ensure a large playing space. Many quick passes and a collective play will ensure the defence will be beaten, thus scoring a goal.

Individual tactical actions when playing defence

While playing defence, all court players should demonstrate their intentions to get possession of the ball, and put pressure on attackers to prevent the throw to goal. Apart from this, players need to ensure they do the following:

Getting back in defence

After losing the ball in attack, all players in the team must get back in defence. The running speed for getting back into defence depends on the way in which the opposing team got possession of the ball. This can be done in the following ways: after scoring a goal, the players will run facing their own goal up to the centre of the court; there, they will try to get as fast as possible to their defence positions in order to face the coming attack. They must also monitor the movement of the opponents on the court, their running direction and the way in which they carry the ball. When the ball is already in possession of the opposite team, players must get back quickly to the centre of the court, without ignoring the man with the ball. It is from there that the defenders will closely mark the most dangerous player – usually the one with the ball or the one closest to the goal – to ensure he is not given an easy scoring opportunity. The opposing attack should find the defenders already well organised within their defensive system.

Launching with the opponent

During a team attack, not all the players should be close to the opposite team's semicircle because a potential fast break would be impossible to stop if the opponents intercept the ball. The attacking players need to ensure the defensive balance is maintained. Certain players have the task of closely guarding the initiators of the fast break – when these players are running, defenders need to move with them; this will determine a timely and safe retreat into defence.

Guarding a direct opponent

The defender must guard a direct opponent and follow the play in all areas of the court. Paying attention is crucial because it leads to an effective collaboration between teammates and creates quick reactions that will slow down or stop the fast break or the second phase of the attack. The defenders who focus only on their direct opponents or on the ball make an incomplete and ineffective contribution to the team defence system, as they limit the activity of only their opponent and not of other attackers who are active in the same area of court.

Intercepting the ball

The defender must be proactive and force their opponents to make mistakes. An interception of the ball can be executed spontaneously and effectively by anticipating the direction of the pass and by the defender placing themselves between two attackers in order to get possession of the ball.

Rebounding the ball

In order to get possession of the ball, defenders must follow the balls thrown towards the goal, or the 7-metre shots saved by the goalkeeper, or those throws that bounce off the post, so they may win the ball on the rebound.

Pressurising and tackling an attacker

This allows the defender to put pressure on an attacker who is throwing the ball to the goal. When trying to block the shot, the defender can also tackle the attacker by blocking the shooting hand and by pushing his hips onto the attacker to prevent him from moving towards the goal. From a tactical perspective, the defender must learn to tell the difference between a fake throw to goal and a proper throw.

Defenders tackling an attacker with the ball

drill 68 step towards attacker with the ball

Objective: To learn how to play in defence and how to step towards the attacker with the ball.

Description: The drill starts with two defenders at the 6-metre semicircle, and two rows of attackers in front of them on the 9-metre semicircle. The attacking players pass the ball between themselves, while the defenders step actively towards the players with the ball before retreating back to the 6-metre semicircle.

Coaching points:
- defenders should have their arms up when they step towards the player with the ball;
- defenders should get back on the 6-metre semicircle as soon as the opposite player with the ball has passed it to his teammate.

Common errors:
- defenders keep their arms low;
- defenders fail to move towards the attacking player as soon as they have the ball.

drill 69 — how to get out to the attacker with the ball

Objective: To learn how to play in defence, and how to step towards the attacker with the ball.

Description: The drill starts with three defenders at the 6-metre semicircle, and three rows of attackers opposite them. The attackers pass the ball while penetrating and retreating, and the defenders step out to the players with the ball before going back to the initial starting position.

Coaching points:
- communicate with teammates when playing in defence;
- make active moves towards the attacker with the ball and use your hands.

Common errors:
- defenders run into the attacking players and make an intentional foul;
- defenders fail to get back on the semicircle quickly enough.

drill 70 6 v 6 defensive drill

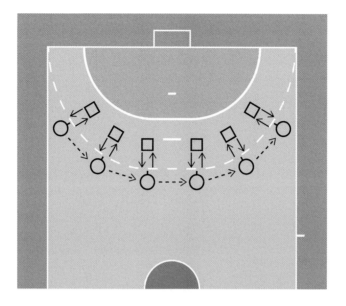

Objective: To learn how to play in defence and how to step towards the attacking player with the ball.

Description: The drill begins with six defenders on the 6-metre semicircle and six attackers who are passing a ball from one wing to the other on the 9-metre semicircle. Each defender is guarding the opponent with the ball by stepping towards him and then moving back onto the semicircle.

Coaching points:
- active use of hands;
- communicate with teammates.

Common errors:
- defenders do not move towards the ball and wait on the 6-metre semicircle;
- defenders do not use their arms.

Objective: To develop defence skills in a 1 v 1 situation and learn how to tackle the attacker.

Description: Two players work with one ball – one attacker and one defender. The player with the ball feints a throw to goal while the defender tries to block the shot by holding his shooting arm.

Coaching point: Defender should place his palm on the attacker's biceps or forearm.

Common error: Defender is too far away from the attacker and because of this cannot block his shooting arm.

switching players in defence

Objective: To learn how to switch players when playing defence.

Description: Two defenders against two attackers with a ball. The player with the ball feints a throw to goal, then executes a simple crossover and changes places with the other attacker; the defenders come to the player with the ball, and then they switch the player they are guarding.

Coaching point: Defenders should say 'switch' when they exchange players.

Common error: Both defenders end up guarding the same player, mainly due to lack of communication.

drill 73 blocking shots at goal

Objective: To learn how to block a shot to goal.

Description: Standing on the 6-metre line, the defenders execute simple moves – sideways, forwards – with their arms stretched overhead, while imitating the action that blocks the ball thrown to goal.

Coaching points:
- have your arms fully extended upwards and keep them fairly close to each other;
- use side steps when moving sideways and do not cross your legs.

Common errors:
- defenders do not have their arms fully extended;
- defenders cross their legs when moving sideways or forwards.

drill 74 blocking shots

Objective: To learn how to block shots.

Description: While jogging around the court, at a signal players jump on both feet while imitating blocking the balls thrown to goal.

Coaching point: Extend your arms upwards and jump at the same time.

Common errors:
- players do not extend their arms upwards;
- players do not jump.

blocking attacker's shooting arm

Objective: To learn how to block the attacker's shooting arm.

Description: Players are in pairs facing each other – one player on the 6-metre semicircle and the other 1-2 metres away. The attacking players have a ball each. The attacker jumps as if he intends to throw to goal, while the defender imitates blocking the ball, by putting one arm on the attacker's shooting hand.

Common errors:
- the defender does not put his arm on the attacker's shooting hand;
- the defender does not get close enough to the attacker who jumps.

drill 76 blocking long–distance shots

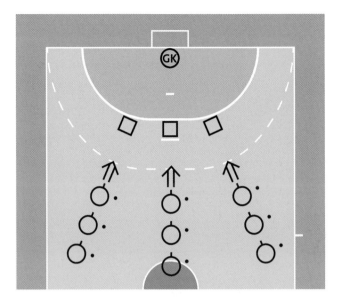

Objective: To practise blocking shots.

Description: Attacking players are grouped in three rows situated at left back, centre back and right back positions about 12 metres from the goal, each of them with a ball. A defender stands in front of each of the three queues at the 6-metre semicircle and one at a time, the attackers execute jump throws to goal, while the defenders block the shots.

Coaching points:
- keep your arms fully extended upwards and fairly close to each other;
- keep an eye on the ball so that you can move your arms to the ball in order to stop it.

Common error: Defenders leave a gap between their arms for the ball to pass through.

drill 77 drill for defence

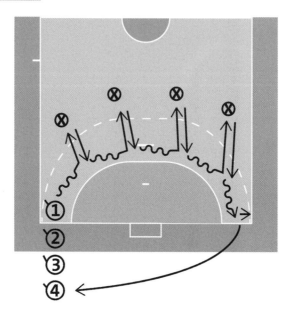

Objective: To practise the basic stance when playing in defence.

Description: Players are lined up in single file at one corner of the court. Player 1 starts the drill by moving sideways (side stepping) from left to right just outside the 6-metre semicircle. When he gets to the cone (placed 9–10 metres from the goal) he sprints towards it with both arms up as if he is blocking a shot; then recovers back to the 6-metre semicircle and continues defensive slides and getting out to stop a shot in front of each cone until he arrives at the other side of the semicircle.

Coaching points:
- use quick and active sideways moves;
- have your arms out, fully extended upwards and sideways;
- sprint towards the cone with both arms up.

Common errors:
- players do not use their arms, but keep their arms low;
- players tend to jump when they move sideways.

Team tactics in defence

The importance of defence and of initiating simple defensive actions even when the team is on offence is emphasised in the modern game. The organisation of the team involves several phases: the re-organisation of the initial attack in case of a failed action (missed shot and getting the offensive rebound for example); organised movement of players from offence back into defence when the attack has failed; organising a temporary defence in own team's half court as a short term strategy when getting back into defence (guarding the goal and preventing the opponents from scoring an easy goal); positioning in defence; and finally implementing a defensive system.

As a team, the first aim after losing possession of the ball is to stop the opponents' fast break. The former attackers – who now become defenders – will try to get the ball back in order to build a new attack, or to stop the fast break initiated by the team that had been in defence, or at least to delay the attack. Each team has its own system of getting back into defence. Occupying the defensive positions begins by taking the shortest path and by assuming responsibility with the main purpose being to avoid receiving a goal, and to win time for all teammates to get back to their defensive positions.

Every defender has several means available to them when playing, including:

- their positioning in defence;
- anticipating opponents' actions – the defenders should think tactically in order to disrupt the attackers' actions;
- switching players and the correct positioning within the defensive system, according to the system used by the attacking team, by respecting several basic rules: the movement of a player should not affect the actions of the others and the technical procedures specific to defence must be used correctly;
- individual and collective actions: guarding the opponent, stealing the ball from the opponent, intercepting the ball, tactical combinations between defenders;
- the rhythm of defence represents the number of actions made during a defensive phase and this may be rapid or slow.

Defence play must be adapted to the opponents' attack and it must also be aggressive and focused on intercepting the ball. The role of each defender is to make the attackers make a mistake, and to get possession of the ball in order to start a new attack. The pressure on the opponent must begin right after losing the ball, by guarding the player with the ball in the area where the fast break is begun, continuing with second phase defence.

The plan to get the ball back from the attacking team must be firm; the player who intervenes in the trajectory of the ball or who attacks the player with the ball will do it using all his energy – this can get very physical at times. The player will aim for the throwing arm, at the same time as the opponent gets the ball. Defender's actions must focus on getting the ball back; this should happen as far as possible from the semicircle, at about 9–12 metres away from the goal. When the ball retrieval begins, the defender will continue to attack the ball carrier until he risks the whistle being blown for a foul. The defender must make any pass difficult, and the defenders must always be moving, covering a large zone, between their own semicircle and beyond the 9-metre line. Arm and leg movements must be a constant concern while in defence.

Another factor in an effective defence is to outnumber the opponents in the zone with the ball, but also paying close attention to the attackers without the ball. All these actions must be carried out at top speed. This requires very good movement from the defender and flexibility from the entire defensive system.

The whole team must ensure they know how to apply the 3:2:1 defence system, with variations to 5:1, 4:2 or 6:0 defence, depending on the demands of the game and on the characteristics of the other team. The team must also be able to switch easily from one defence system to another.

During the game, defenders have certain specific collective tactics which they should employ depending on the stage the game is at. These are:

- counting and allocating the opponents: each defender has to guard an attacker who acts in his line area;
- speaking in defence – when the attacking team begins tactical combinations and modify their positions, the defenders must communicate the path of the attackers to each other;
- sliding – when a defender follows a direct opponent and goes in front or behind the back of a teammate (specific to man-to-man defence);

Defending actions can be very physical

- switching players – this refers to changing opponents and guarding an attacker currently being marked by a teammate. This usually happens when an attacker threatens the goal and modifies his position following a tactical combination – the defender who initially guards this attacker will shout 'switch' so that a teammate who is better placed will now guard that attacker;
- closing the corridors – when two defenders come shoulder to shoulder in order to reduce the penetration space toward the goal;
- wall and mutual help – when the defender goes to the attacker with the ball and redistributes the space left between the defenders next to him, depending on the direction of the ball;
- getting back– getting back on to the 6-metre semicircle after going to the attacker with the ball;
- replacing – the tactical action used by defenders as a way to cover the space left open by a teammate who gets out of position.

Playing systems in defence

Different defensive systems are employed for particular attacking systems, and vice versa. Most of the time, the defence adapts and adjusts to the specific attack and to the strengths of the attacking players, also taking into account their own strengths and their tactical experience. For defence play, teams use systems that evolved alongside the development of the handball game. Thus, the game comprises several systems of defence: zone, man-to-man and combined defence. Each defensive system has advantages and disadvantages.

Zone defence

Each defender has to monitor or cover a certain area of the court, where any opponent that comes into that area is guarded closely, preventing him from moving towards the goal or throwing to goal. The defender guards the opponent as long as he is in his defence zone/area of responsibility. The defender follows the attacker until he gets out of his zone and this is when another defender starts guarding him. The zone defence is characterised by movement, determined by the location and direction of the opponents' attack; it is executed in front of the semicircle by all the defenders. The shifting – a sideways movement on the 6-metre line – is also accompanied by successive forward moves by the defenders.

It is necessary to be aggressive (within limits set by the rules) and to attack the player with the ball when they are in a position to throw to goal. The free space within the defence line caused by this move forward is covered by the shift of the two closest teammates. Zone defence is quite difficult because the players must synchronise their actions to adapt to the attacking actions. Actions such as mutual help, guarding the opponents, giving up on the defensive line and approaching another opponent who is more dangerous are only some tasks required of the defenders.

The 6:0 zone defence system

All six defenders are placed at the 6-metre semicircle or right in front of it, in one line, with gaps of 2–3 metres between them. They are meant to cover as much as possible of the semicircle area. If an opponent threatens the goal or is about to throw to goal, then the defender who is in that zone will advance, putting the attacker under pressure, and will attempt to block the throw or to tackle. The 6:0 defence is used against teams that do not have strong backs and that focus their play on combinations with the pivots. This playing system is generally used by women's teams and juniors.

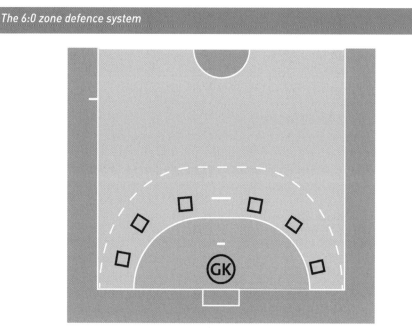

The 6:0 zone defence system

The 5:1 zone defence system

This defensive system can be used against teams that rely on plentiful activity from the backs and of the line players. On the 6-metre line, the team has five defenders that can cover a significant part of the court, and in front of them in the free-throw area another defender is placed, whose main task is to prevent the opponents from making long throws in the central zone of the court – see below. This defender's position on the court allows interception of passes to change the direction of the attack. The 5+1 defence is vulnerable to the attacking system with two pivots.

The 4:2 zone defence system

This defence system is characterised by the following positioning on the court: four defenders at the 6-metre semicircle and the other two in the free-throw area. Initially, these two players defend the centre of the court where goals are scored easily. The four defenders at the 6-metre semicircle have to cover wide areas of the court. In order to stop potential penetrations, they will have to replace one another continuously. If the two defenders that are advanced do not move efficiently, large spaces will be created at the 6-metre line and the actions of the opposite wings and of the pivot will become more difficult to stop.

The 3:2:1 defence

The 3:2:1 is an advanced defensive system, specific to teams that have a good fitness level and it is used against an attack with a strong 9-metre line presence. The positioning is as follows: the pivot will guard the opponents' pivot, the wings monitor their direct opponents at the 9-metre line, while the backs and the centre back will be far up in defence at 9-10 metres.

Man-to-man defence

In the modern game of handball, the man-to-man defence is used rarely, as it requires a very active movement from the defenders, good communication and generally a good fitness level. Two situations when this system is used are: when the opposing team uses a slow positional play and attempts to prolong the attack without losing the ball; or when the aim is to surprise the opponent and to get him out of the attacking system which was initially planned.

Combined defence

There are several forms of combined defence in which one or several players apply the principles and rules of man-to-man defence, while the other players use zone defence principles.

defence when outnumbering the opponents

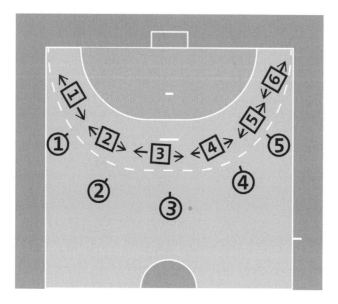

Objective: To learn to defend with an extra player.

Description: Used following the suspension of an opposite player. Five defenders will guard five attackers and they play man-to-man, while the sixth defender goes to the 6-metre line, where he will act as safety player. In most cases, the team in defence goes to the 6-metre semicircle, plays in a line and will move depending on the direction of the other team passing the ball, without advancing toward the opponent and thus focusing on closing the corridors.

Coaching points:
- focus on closing the corridors – minimise the gap between defenders;
- defence should move in time with the ball.

Common errors:
- defenders do not move when the ball moves;
- lack of communication between defenders.

defence when outnumbered by the opponents

Objective: To learn how to play in defence when a player down.

Description: Used following the suspension of a teammate. The team should go to the 6-metre line fast, in order to avoid creating corridors by advancing toward the opponent. The man-to-man defence is not used because the possibility arises for the unguarded attacker to create a scoring opportunity or score a goal. An outnumbered defence can also occur as a consequence of a fast break by the opposite team – in this situation the defenders will try to slow down the offence so that their teammates have time to get back in defence.

Coaching point: Avoid playing man-to-man defence in this situation and focus on principles of zone defence.

Common errors:
- players do not stay on the 6-metre semicircle;
- players guard an opposing player instead of playing in the zone.

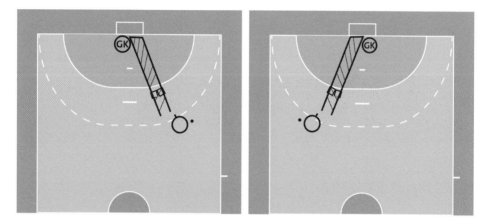

drill 80 defending throws

Objective: To practise defending against throws with the wall.

Description: Depending on the throwing arm and on the spot where this throw is executed from, the wall formed by the defenders will cover either the long or the short corner – see above. The goalkeeper will always place themselves in the right corner of the goal – see above left – if the throw is executed by a right-handed player and in the left corner of the goal if the shooter is left-handed. The defenders within the wall must attempt to block the throws of the opponents. Those who block the 9-metre throws must respond only to throws, not to fake throws.

Common errors:
- players do not stay close enough together when making the wall;
- players do not have their arms fully extended upwards.

THE GOALKEEPER

Goalkeeper technique and skills

The goalkeeper technique in handball is complex and takes time to learn. The aim is to defend the goal, and initiate any attack. In the following pages, the technical elements that a goalkeeper needs to master will be discussed:

- Goalkeeper stance;
- Goalkeeper movements;
- Catching the ball;
- Saving shots;
- Launch the fast break.

Goalkeeper stance

A good goalkeeper stance means adopting a position from which they are ready to move in any direction with maximum speed. So the basic start position of the keeper is how the hands, trunk and legs are positioned. The arms are open, hands need to be in line with the arms, level with the shoulders with palms facing forward and with all fingers spread out; legs should be open and in line with the shoulders; heels off the ground and knees slightly bent.

Goalkeeper fundamental position

The goalkeeper stance can be adjusted to the angle of shooting, so if a player is shooting from the right or left wing the keeper position changes. The intention of covering the short corner and the long corner can be seen from the position of both arms: with one hand above head for the short corner and the other arm as a diagonal extension of the body for the long corner – as can be seen below. Some goalkeepers have their own style and prefer to move forward diagonally from the bar so they can decrease the angle of the wing player who is trying to score.

Goalkeeper covering the short and long corner

Goalkeeper decreasing the angle of the wing player trying to score

Goalkeeper movements

Basic goalkeeper movements consist of short steps performed laterally. Usually, the goalkeeper moves along the line in front of the goal and the direction of the movement is determined by the attackers' passes. The steps are shorter and slower, but the line of movement can be different – for example movement line A – close to goal line – or line B – in a semicircle shape in front of goal line – as can be seen below.

Goalkeepers need to maintain a consistent distance between their feet and keep their knees slightly bent for a springier move. This will allow the goalkeeper to quickly jump forward, stop quickly and then jump back to the previous position and continue the movement in any dangerous situation – as illustrated below.

Goalkeeper movement line in front of his goal

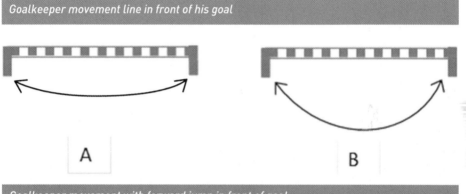

A

B

Goalkeeper movement with forward jump in front of goal

Catching the ball

In handball it is recommended that all players, including the goalkeeper when the situation permits, catch the ball with two hands all the time. While it is easy for the field players to catch the ball after a pass, for the keeper it is harder because players are using their whole power to try to score. Therefore it is important for the keeper to stay in his basic position and wait to catch the ball with two hands: have both hands in front of his face with all fingers open wide and thumbs close to each other ready for the ball – see below.

Goalkeeper catching the ball with both hands

Sometimes balls can be thrown higher or lower so the keeper needs to be ready to move in the right direction: if the ball is coming high the goalkeeper will use a slight jump with both hands up in the air ready to catch the ball; if the ball is placed in the middle of the goal the keeper needs to push on his legs and to move both hands ready to save the goal. If the ball is placed very low then the keeper can either dive for the ball like a football goalkeeper would do – or move with one leg straight on the ground and the other leg bent at the knee, almost like performing the splits – see page 143.

Goalkeeper catching a ball coming high

Goalkeeper saving the ball from the middle of the goal

Goalkeeper performing a diving save

Goalkeeper saving a low ball

Saving shots

Goal defence is the most obvious technique used by handball goalkeepers. During training sessions the goalkeeper should be taught different defence techniques, starting with the most basic and going through to the more difficult, so he can experience both. The main aim is for the keeper to use different techniques in order to surprise an attacker – this will give more chances to save the goal in a one-to-one situation.

Saving technique for high shots

The best and safest way of saving high shots is with both hands and this technique must be taught from the very first session. Having said that, sometimes in the top games goalkeepers use only one hand – it all depends on the goalkeeper's experience and the position he was in when the shot was executed.

As it can be seen below, when saving high shots the goalkeeper needs to hop on one leg and have both hands extended above the head as an extension of the body; it is a short jump for the short corner and a long jump for trying to save a ball in the long corner. The faster and more energetic the jump is, the more successful is the action.

Goalkeeper saving technique for high shots

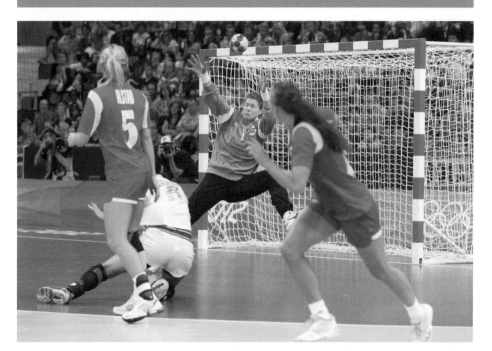

Saving technique for low shots

Some differences can be noticed when defending these types of shots – it all depends on what the goalkeeper has learned and practised, and personal choice during the match. The most used technique is the slide on one side with the hand in front of the bent leg. The goalkeeper steps sideways with one leg bent and the other one straight. At the same time as the leg action, the goalkeeper will place his hand in front of the bent leg while the other arm will be kept either above his head or extended sideways, as illustrated ibelow.

Another technique for saving low shots is with straight legs. This technique is used by goalkeepers with more experience and at a higher level. From a very low position the goalkeeper parts his legs until almost sitting on the floor with legs straight performing the splits. One hand is in front of the leg extended trying to save the ball while the other one is placed above the hip area, as illustrated opposite.

Goalkeeper saving technique for low shots

Saving medium high shots

In this situation the goalkeeper should save the ball with his hands, or with a leg and hand at the same time. The most popular technique is step-in saving – this is when the goalkeeper steps in towards the ball raising a straight hand in the direction of the ball with the trunk stretched.

When the goalkeeper is standing a distance from the place where the ball is heading, he can use both hand and leg at the same time – the goalkeeper will place his arm next to the elevated foot – helping to increase the chance of saving the shot during the action.

Goalkeeper saving a shot using his arms and legs

Another common technique is the star jump, or butterfly jump.

This technique is used by goalkeepers with experience and is very efficient in one-to-one situations in the semicircle area, and also when the referee has awarded a penalty shot from the 7-metre line. Using this technique, the goalkeeper is trying to intimidate the player and has more chance of saving the ball. The goalkeeper is moving forward, jumping up in the air, stretching both arms and legs straight, making his body as big as possible in an attempt to cover an area of the goal that is as wide as possible.

Goalkeeper using a star jump to save the ball

Launching the fast break

The goalkeeper is the player who needs to put the ball back in the game after the opposite team has lost possession while trying to score. Certain skills are required to be able to pass the ball as precisely and accurately as possible, on time and to the right teammate. If the goalkeeper has decided to pass the ball to the nearest player, who is normally the centre player, then the defenders have more time to go back to their defending areas. That is why the goalkeeper needs to be quick and looking forward for the wings, who are normally the first ones to run towards the attacking area, to be able to launch the fast break and score easy and quickly.

A very simple technique should be employed to launch the counterattack – just an over-arm throw which every single player in a handball team should be able to execute. Some goalkeepers use short lateral steps before sending the fast break pass to get more power into the throw, while other keepers use cross steps, as can be seen on the next page.

Goalkeeper using lateral steps before launcing the fast break

Goalkeeper using lateral steps before launcing the fast break

Goalkeeper using cross steps before launching the fast break

Goalkeeper tactics

As well as technique, tactics must hold the same importance, or even more, if you think that the goalkeeper is the one who needs to take a quick and correct decision in order to be able to save as many goals as possible, to collaborate with the team regarding the defence and to be able to launch a fast break so the team can score as quick as possible. Tasks and actions performed by the goalkeeper are not confined only to saving the goals from the opposite team; he participates in the defence, organising defenders and communicating with them all the time during the game.

The major components of goalkeeper tactics are the position of the goalkeeper depending on the player who is throwing; the communication between the goalkeeper and defenders; stopping the counterattack and the launch of the counterattack.

The position: A goalkeeper needs to know how to react in different ways depending on the position and type of throw. So if the attacker throws from a long range shot (9-metre line) – the goalkeeper needs to quickly analyse the attacker's position. Sometimes the goalkeeper can force the attacker to throw to a particular area of the goal depending on the way he is moving, so that is why it is very important for the goalkeeper to know how and when to move. He needs to trust his teammates and to at least partly move out of the block area to see the situation and be able to save the throw.

Goalkeeper positioning when defending long range shots (from the 9 metre line)

Short range shot (6-metre line) – for this type of shooting the goalkeeper needs to be brave and courageous as the attacker is within a short distance and potentially shooting from a small angle. In this situation the goalkeeper is moving inside the goal area so is able to block a greater area of the goal and should be always moving in the same direction as the player with the ball.

One-to-one situation – this is the time when the field player has time to see what the goalkeeper is going to do. So if the goalkeeper is passive and concentrates on the shooter, he has the chance to save the throw; if he leaves his hands down then he can provoke the field player to throw the ball in a different direction. It all depends on the experience of each goalkeeper and their own style. Some goalkeepers use a jump with hands and legs out so they can cover more of the corners, while others will use fake movements, depending on the attacker position.

7-metre free throw (penalty) – in this situation the attacker has three seconds to release the ball at which time he can throw straight to the goal, or can make a fake move with the ball or with the body, so the goalkeeper needs to keep his attention fully focused on the hand with the ball. Having his knees bent and hands up in the ready position, he is able to react in the moment the ball is released from the player's hand. Depending on the individual, goalkeepers can use two different types of position in the goal: either adopting the position on the goal line, when he can choose the direction of the action , as seen below, or standing on the 4m line – in this situation he makes the angle smaller and the field player needs to be more precise; the attacker has the chance to throw the ball over the goalkeeper, but at the same time the player can be intimidated by the goalkeeper movements – see page 149.

Goalkeeper defending a 7 metre throw from the goal line

The communication between the goalkeeper and defenders is important to achieve maximum efficiency in goal defence. The defenders must take into account the goalkeeper's skills and technique and it is important to have a good relationship between them. The first task of the defender is trying to block the shot on goal. As a matter of principle it is established that the defender will try to cover the short corner and so the goalkeeper has to move towards the long corner. The situation is even more complicated when the attacker is guarded by more than one defender; if the defenders' action is from each side of the attacker, they are trying to cover each of the corners. If they are forming a pair – they are trying to cover the short corner leaving the long one for the goalkeeper (see page 151). A different situation is when a 9-metre player is trying to shoot and there are two players defending the shot and a third defender trying to stop the shooter from sideways. In this situation the two defenders are covering most of the goal area and the third one is trying to make the throwing action difficult so the goalkeeper has more chance to save. It's very important for the goalkeeper to guide the defenders in the right direction, making his job easier as well as theirs.

Communication between defender and goalkeeper

Two defenders covering the short and long corner

Two defenders covering the short corner while the goalkeeper covers the long corner

Two defenders covering the goal area while a third defender attempts to block the shot

Stopping the counterattack is one of the most important tasks of the goalkeeper as they are the first and the last defender of the team. When his team is attacking, the goalkeeper is allowed to come out of the 6-metre semicircle and to help his team by stopping the counterattack from the opposite team – he waits between the 7-metre line and the 9-metre semicircle, ready to intercept the ball in case of a fast break. He needs to be alert in case of an unsuccessful attack so he can return as quickly as possible to his area to coordinate his teammates. So his role is to make it difficult or even impossible for the opposite team to pass the ball or to take possession of the ball. Another situation when the goalkeeper's role is important is when his teammates have no one to pass to while on offence – the goalkeeper may come out of the semicircle area to receive the pass and to help the attack continue.

Launch the counterattack – the success of the counterattack involves an essential contribution from the goalkeeper during the early stages of his team attack. This task is not easy at all, and needs lots of practising together with certain skills: the power of throwing, excellent precision, quick and accurate calculation of speed and direction of the player launched for the counterattack. If the goalkeeper is able to pass the ball quickly and precisely to the player who is sprinting on the fast break, then the action can be successful.

Generally speaking the ideal zones where a teammate is supposed to receive the ball are in the opposite team area, after the half way line and just before the 9-metre semicircle, so that after receiving the ball he has time to make 2–3 steps to get into the semicircle where he can shoot and score. When there are no players in that area, then the goalkeeper has to decide where he is going to send the first pass to make the fast break quicker and have more chances to score. It all depends on the teammate's direction and position, so the goalkeeper has to analyse quickly and precisely who is the best person to receive the ball and to continue the second phase of the offence. The best areas for the goalkeeper to launch the counterattack are illustrated below.

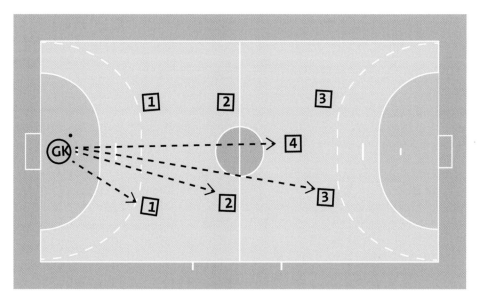

Drills and exercises for goalkeeper training

Like any other sport, the warm-up has a very important role in handball. For the goalkeeper a very specific warm-up has to be performed. The simplest exercises include basic gymnastics movements which contribute to the general development of the body.

Some of the most common static and dynamic stretches for a goalkeeper warm-up include:

- from a standing position: rotate your arms in circles (10 forwards and 10 backwards) and then try to alternate the direction – one arm forward, the other one backwards at the same time;
- from a standing position with legs a shoulder width apart: hold your hands together over your head extending your body, bend your body trying to touch your toes and then go back to the start position;
- from a standing position with legs crossed over (one in front of the other): try to touch your toes and stay there for 15–20 seconds; if you had your left leg over your right leg next time switch over;
- side lunges, left and right;
- sitting down with legs wide open: bend your trunk forward trying to reach forward as far as you can and stay there for 15–20 seconds, then alternate bending your body towards your left leg and then to your right;
- lying on the floor: roll back and bring your legs above your head and then go back to the starting position; repeat a couple of times;
- attempt to perform the splits.

drill 81 saving high shots

Objective: To practise saving shots coming high.

Description: From the basic stance position, in the centre of the goal, the goalkeeper jumps up to the top right corner, coming back to the start position and then jumps up to the top left corner and back to centre again. Repeat 5 times to each corner.

Coaching points:
- ensure you jump with arms up, fully extended;
- try to assess the direction of the shot.

Common errors:
- goalkeeper does not jump;
- goalkeeper does not extend his arms.

saving low shots

Objective: To practise saving shots coming low.

Description: From the basic stance position, in the centre of the goal, the goalkeeper moves to the bottom right corner using a lunge with the right hand in front of his right foot and the left arm above his head. Come back to the start position and do exactly the same to the left corner. Repeat 5 times to each corner.

Coaching points:
- use the right arm and right foot at the same time when going to save the ball;
- recover quickly, back to the middle of the goal from the lunge position.

Common errors:
- the goalkeeper does not use his right arm and his right foot at exactly the same time;
- the goalkeeper does not anticipate correctly the direction of the ball;
- the goalkeeper does not recover quickly enough back to the middle of the goal.

drill 83 saving different shots 1

Objective: To practise saving shots coming from various heights.

Description: From the basic stance position, in the centre of the goal, now alternate the previous two exercises: jump up to the top right corner and then come back to the centre of the goal and then go down in a lunge to the left corner and back again into the initial starting position. Repeat 5 times to each corner.

Coaching point: Jump high or lunge powerfully to the side when defending the shot.

Common errors:
- the goalkeeper does not have his arms extended;
- the goalkeeper fails to recover quickly enough back to the middle of the goal.

drill 84   saving different shots 2

Objective: To practise saving shots coming from various heights.

Description: Same as previous drill, but this time lunge down to the right corner, going back to the start position and then jump up to the top left corner. Repeat 5 times to each corner.

Coaching points:
- jump high or lunge powerfully to the side when saving the ball;
- keep your arms extended;
- recover quickly to the middle of the goal.

Common errors:
- the goalkeeper does not keep his arms extended;
- the goalkeeper does not recover quickly enough back to the middle of the goal after saving a shot.

drill 85 training without the ball 1

Objective: To learn the basic moves in goal.

Description: From the basic stance position, in the centre of the goal, the goalkeeper pretends to save a goal by moving his right leg and right arm at the same time as high as he can. Repeat 5 times. Change to do exactly the same for the other leg and arm (repeating 5 times).

Coaching points:
- actions need to be performed quickly – right arm and right leg at the same time;
- recover to the starting position immediately.

Common errors:
- arm and leg do not move at the same time;
- goalkeeper keeps his arm and leg extended for too long instead of recovering quickly back to the initial stance.

training without the ball 2

Objective: To learn the basic moves in goal.

Description: Same as drill 85, but this time with alternate directions: one move to the right followed by one to the left.

Coaching points:
- all actions must be performed quickly, with arm and leg moved at the same time;
- be on your toes and maintain a balanced position between each move.

Common errors:
- movement of arm and leg is slow;
- player's balance is lost while performing the moves.

It is worth mentioning that if the team has two goalkeepers it is recommended they work as a pair, facing each other, as if in a mirror. For professional players a bench can be introduced on the goal line, in the middle of the 6-metre semicircle, and they can execute all the exercises mentioned above while jumping over the bench. When using a ball, one goalkeeper should do the drills and the other should throw the ball to his partner. In case of a team that does not have two goalkeepers, the coach can help out, or even one of the teammates.

pass to the partner

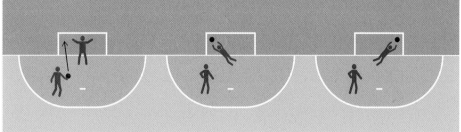

Objective: To practise basic saving moves.

Description: The goalkeeper stands in the middle of the goal, adopting the basic stance position; his partner with a handball in his hands is situated in front of him at about 1–2 metres away and throws the ball up to the right corner. The goalkeeper needs to catch the ball with both hands, passing back to him then going back to the middle ready to receive the ball up to the left corner this time. Five executions on each side and then the goalkeepers change roles.

Coaching points:
- the goalkeeper needs to start the drill in the basic 'ready' stance;
- use both hands to catch the ball.

Common error: Goalkeeper is not in the middle of the goal.

goalkeepers working in pairs 1

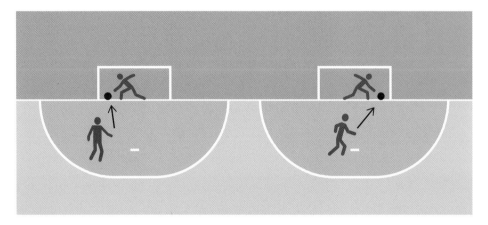

Objective: To practise basic goalkeeper moves.

Description: The same starting position as drill 87, but this time the other goalkeeper will throw the handball down to the corners. From the basic stance position in the middle of the goal, the goalkeeper will bend down through a lunge, catching the ball, passing back to his teammate, going back to the start position and doing it again to the other corner. Five executions on each side and then the goalkeepers change roles.

Coaching points:
- moves need to be fast, and as low as possible;
- start each time from the basic stance position.

Common errors:
- goalkeeper does not start from the basic stance position;
- goalkeeper does not bend down as low as possible to save the shot.

goalkeepers working in pairs 2

Objective: To practise goalkeeper saving moves.

Description: After drills 87 and 88 the goalkeepers can alternate: throwing one ball up to the right corner, waiting for the goalkeeper to go back in the centre of the goal and then throwing down to the left corner and then swap: down right and up left. Five executions on each side and then the goalkeepers change roles.

Coaching points:
- make quick sharp moves each time the ball is thrown;
- recover to the middle of the goal after each save.

Common errors:
- goalkeeper reacts too slowly after the ball is thrown;
- goalkeeper does not get back in the middle of the goal.

The next set of drills involves the whole team working just for the goalkeepers.

drill 90 single file shooting

Objective: To practise basic saving moves.

Description: The goalkeeper stands in the basic stance position in the middle of the goal while the whole team is situated in single file with a handball each behind the 7-metre line. They will throw the balls at shoulder level one after another into the goalkeeper's hands. This time the goalkeeper's job is not to catch the ball but to shove the ball back, away from him, trying to protect his face at the same time, and then get ready for the next shot.

Coaching points:
- use both hands to shove the balls away;
- be on your toes and maintain a well balanced position in the middle of goal.

Common errors:
- the goalkeeper does not use both hands;
- field players throw the ball too low or to the side.

drill 91 high shot saving

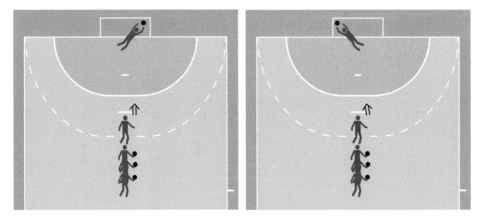

Objective: To practise saving shots that come high.

Description: The goalkeeper stands in the basic stance position in the middle of the goal. His teammates are behind the 7-metre line in single file with a handball each, ready to throw the ball up to the corners for the goalkeeper to save these shots. The first player throws to the top left corner and the next one throws to the opposite top corner and so on. When performing this drill, the players need to wait for the goalkeeper to return to the middle of the goal so he has time to save every single ball. Once again it is very important for the goalkeeper not to try to catch the ball but to shove the ball away.

Coaching points:
- do not catch the ball – try to shove it away;
- get back in the middle of the goal using the basic stance position.

Common errors:
- goalkeeper catches the ball;
- attackers do not throw the ball where they are supposed to – high, to the top corners.

drill 92 low shot saving

Objective: To practise saving shots that come low.

Description: Exactly the same as drill 91, but this time the players need to throw the ball down to the corners, alternately right and left. It is important for the player to concentrate and see exactly where the person in front of him has thrown so he knows where to throw his shot.

Coaching points:
- use quick powerful moves with side lunges;
- get back into the middle of the goal in the basic stance position.

Common errors:
- goalkeeper moves too slowly back into the middle of the goal after saving a shot;
- attackers do not throw the ball where they are supposed to.

alternate shot saving

Objective: To practise saving various different shots.

Description: The same as drill 91, but this time they will alternate the shooting: one up to the left corner and one down to the right corner. After all players have finished shooting, change to: one shot down to the left corner and one up to the right corner. Same rule applies – shooting players need to wait for the goalkeeper to come back into the middle of the goal.

Coaching points:
- make quick sharp moves from one side of the goal to the other;
- get back to the middle of the goal and maintain a well balanced position.

Common errors:
- slow moves between the saves;
- goalkeeper loses his balance.

After all these standard warm-up exercises the goalkeeper is ready to defend more challenging shots coming from different positions.

drill 94 saving shots from the wing

Objective: To practise saving shots from the wings.

Description: The team can be split into two groups: one group is shooting from the left wing and the other group from the right wing, each player with a ball. If the drill starts from the left wing you need to alternate: one shot from the left and then one from the right, while giving enough time for the goalkeeper to move from one side to another. You can continue with this type of exercise, moving the players from one position to another, from wings to intermediary, to centre and to semicircle players.

Coaching points:
- when the shot from the wing is coming, the goalkeeper needs to be as close to the post as possible;
- attackers should allow for the goalkeeper to move from one side to the other.

Common error: Goalkeeper leaves a gap between him and the goal, so attackers can score.

fast break for goalkeeper and one attacker

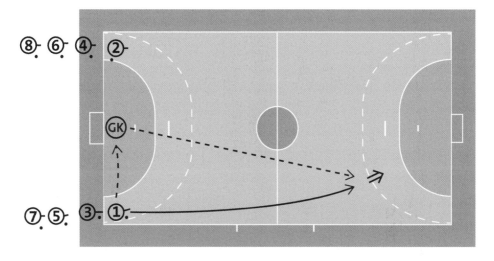

Objective: To practise launching a good counterattack.

Description: Same set up as drill 94. Each player needs to pass the ball to the goalkeeper and then run towards the other half of the court. When the runner is at the 9-metre semicircle the goalkeeper passes the ball back to him.

Coaching points:
- the accuracy of the pass is important;
- catch the ball with both hands.

Common errors:
- the pass from the goalkeeper is not accurate;
- the attacker drops the ball.

fast break with a pass from intermediary position

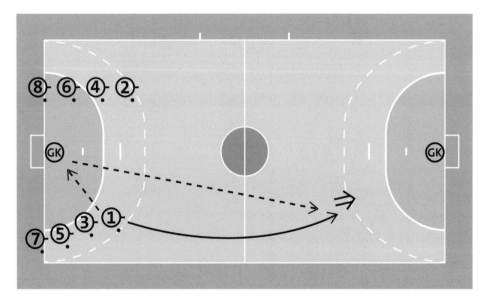

Objective: To rehearse launching a fast break with a pass from the intermediary position.

Description: Same set up as drill 94. This time the players are passing the balls from the intermediary position – alternating from left to right and so on. The goalkeeper needs to concentrate on the precision of passing the ball and to analyse the speed of the player so he can pass the ball to the right place at the right time.

Coaching points:
- accuracy of passing is important;
- players should catch the ball with both hands.

Common errors:
- the goalkeeper does not anticipate correctly the speed of the player and sends a bad pass;
- players do not catch the ball with both hands.

drill 97 7-metre throw

Objective: To practise 7-metre throws and saving shots.

Description: Towards the end of the training session, the team can practise throwing from the 7-metre line. This is a very good practice for all the players including the goalkeeper. The goalkeeper can choose his own saving technique: either waiting on the line of the goal or moving forward towards the 4-metre mark. You can play this drill in the form of a simple competition: if one of the players manages to score then the next one in the queue has to score as well, otherwise he is out and so on. The drill continues until there is only one player left and the competition winner is decided between that player and the goalkeeper – if the goalkeeper manages to save the ball then he is the winner; if the player scores then he becomes the winner.

Coaching points:
- the goalkeeper needs to develop an appreciation for the ball trajectory;
- quick and sharp reactions when moving to save the shot.

Common error: The goalkeeper fails to react when the shot is being taken.

drill 98 — saving shots outside the goalkeeper's area

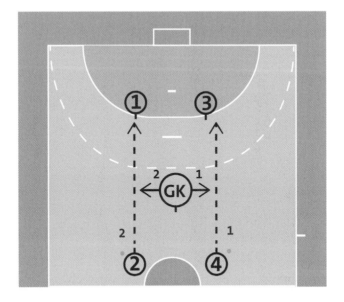

Objective: To practise saving shots.

Description: For this drill the goalkeeper will work with four field players who are in pairs facing each other about 3–4 metres away. Player 4 passes to Player 3 and the goalkeeper will aim to shove the ball away. Afterwards, the goalkeeper comes back to the starting place and will try to do the same with the ball passed by Player 2 towards Player 1. The goalkeeper will continue to intercept the ball when Player 1 passes back to Player 2, and when Player 3 passes back to Player 4 and so on.

Coaching points:
- the goalkeeper should always keep an eye on the ball;
- use one or both arms to save the ball.

Progression: The field players can use a bounce pass and the goalkeeper will use side lunges to shove the ball away.

drill 99 goalkeeper reaction

Objective: To develop quick reactions.

Description: Three field players each with a ball, face the goalkeeper and throw their balls one at a time at the wall behind the goalkeeper. At the moment of the throw, the goalkeeper needs to turn quickly and catch the ball that is bouncing off the wall so that the ball does not touch the floor.

Coaching points:
- be ready to catch the ball;
- make a quick turn to catch the ball bouncing off the wall.

Common errors:
- goalkeeper is slow in turning around;
- goalkeeper does not have his arms ready to catch the ball.

drill 100 goalkeeper v field players

Objective: To develop saving technique.

Description: Two goalkeepers and six field players take part in this drill. The goalkeepers' task is to touch and deflect with any part of their body the two balls that are being passed at the same time by the six players who are placed in a circle.

Coaching points:
- goalkeepers need to have their arms ready and be on their toes;
- goalkeepers need to anticipate the direction of the pass.

Progression: The ball can be kicked between the passing players instead.

save the shot and run around the cone

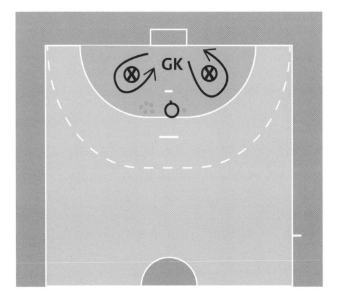

Objective: To practise saving shots and moving fast when in goal.

Description: One player has several balls ready to throw to the goal from a short distance. The goalkeeper will save the shots and will have to run around a cone that is situated 2–3 metres away inside the semicircle, after each save he makes.

Coaching points:
- save the shot and run quickly around the cone;
- the player throwing the ball must alternate the shots – low, high, powerful, etc.

Progression:
- each player throws two shots in a row;
- the goalkeeper must go around both cones after each save, or after each goal is scored.

These exercises and drills are basic ones that goalkeepers should manage in training sessions. Depending on experience, coaches can add more advanced drills to develop the techniques and tactics required to play at a high level.

USEFUL WEBSITES

www.eurohandball.com
The official website of the European Handball Federation, the governing body of handball in Europe.

www.frh.ro
The official website of the Romanian Handball Federation.

www.ihf.info
The official website of the International Handball Federation, the governing body of handball at world level.

www.olympic.org
The official website of the International Olympic Committee – a very good resource for all Olympic sports.

www.englandhandball.com
The official website of England Handball, the governing body of handball in England.

www.britishhandball.com
The official website of British Handball, the governing body of handball in Great Britain.

www.scottishhandball.com
The official website of Scottish Handball, the governing body of handball in Scotland.

APPENDIX

Referees' signals

Reproduced with kind permission from IHF.

1   *Entering the goal area*

2   *Illegal dribble*

3   *Too many steps or holding the ball more than three seconds*

4   *Restraining, holding or pushing*

5 *Hitting*   **6** *Offensive foul*

7 *Throw-in – direction*   **8** *Goalkeeper-throw*

9 *Free-throw – direction*

10 *Keep the distance of 3 meters*

11 *Passive play*

12 *Goal*

13 *Warning (yellow)*
Disqualification (red)

14 *Suspension (2 minutes)*

15 *Time-out*

16 *Permission for two person who are*
'entitled to participate' to enter the court
during time-out

17 *Forewaring signal for passive play*